SOLVING MATHS PROBLEMS

for ages 7-9

Andrew Brodie ✔

Contents

Introduction *3*

Introduction

It is widely recognised that there is a need for activities that address 'using and applying mathematics' through solving problems. However 'using and applying' should be exactly that. Children can only use and apply what they already know and this should include a strong grasp of number as well as knowledge of appropriate techniques and mathematical vocabulary.

In *Solving Maths Problems* we encourage the development of number skills and calculation techniques and the application of these skills to problem-solving situations. All aspects of 'using and applying mathematics' are covered through the wide range of activities in this series.

It is important to consider what we mean by the term 'problem' in mathematics. A problem can consist of a question presented in words, requiring children to 'decode' the question then to decide which mathematical processes to apply. It can also mean any mathematical activity that requires children to investigate, following logical processes. Some problems are, of course, 'closed' – a question is presented to the children and there is only one answer to the question, but the child has to make decisions over which mathematical skills to use and how to follow these through. Other problems are 'open-ended', giving children the opportunity to investigate further. This series provides a variety of both 'closed' and 'open-ended' problems.

In this book you will find several pages featuring the same type of problem. This allows for revision of techniques already learnt but also for further attempts at problems that may have presented difficulties the first time round. It is very important that children should not feel defeated by maths when they make errors – instead they should be encouraged to learn from their mistakes and to 'have another go' at a similar problem.

How to use this book
The first 59 activity sheets in this book are targeted towards Year 3. Activity sheets 60-118 are targeted towards Year 4. However, you can use any of the activity sheets with your own class, regardless of which year group you have, dependent on ability. The children must have the necessary levels of skill in number work to be able to tackle the questions posed on each activity sheet – you will need to decide which children are ready for each activity. The aim should be for children to be engaged in enjoyable activities that provide practice of mathematical skills and knowledge.

You will find that some activities are visited more than once, but using different numbers or quantities, so that children can gain repeated practice of the problem-solving skills.

Some of the sheets can be used independently, with just a small amount of support. These sheets may include 'word problems' where the questions require the children to make decisions on how to solve the problems posed. The children will gain confidence in dealing with these types of problems once they have experienced the 'discussion problems' that are also featured.

The **teachers' notes** on each activity sheet offer a suggested objective for the activity. Most sheets offer opportunities to address a wide range of objectives and you might decide to concentrate on a completely different objective, again centred on the needs of your own class. A problem is then posed. On some sheets there are also extension problems for more able children.

All of the activity sheets can also be found on the **accompanying CD-ROM** for you to print out or display on a whiteboard for group discussion. You might also decide to print out and laminate specific activity sheets for repeated use. In this way you can quickly build a bank of resources for stimulating discussion of maths and for setting problems. Answers to the activities are also on the CD-ROM where appropriate.

Assessment
Pages 4-9 feature guidelines for assessing mathematics, based on the Assessment Guidelines provided through the National Strategies. They are presented in the form of questions. You could choose to use these pages as individual record sheets - highlighting each question in green when you feel the child has a high level of achievement, in orange when you feel that the pupil is secure, and in red if you feel that the child has a low level of achievement. Alternatively, you could tick the box beside statements that you feel the child is secure in the skills specified.

Guidelines for assessing mathematics
<u>Level 1</u>

Using and applying mathematics
Pupils use mathematics as an integral part of classroom activities. They represent their work with objects or pictures and discuss it. They recognise and use a simple pattern or relationship.

- Do the children use mathematics as an integral part of classroom activities, eg with support? Do the children engage with practical mathematical activities involving sorting, counting and measuring by direct comparison? (Ma1 Level 1) ❏

- Do the children represent their work with objects or pictures? Do the children discuss their work? Do the children respond to questions and ideas from peers and adults? Do the children refer to the materials they have used and talk about what they have done, patterns they have noticed, etc? (Ma1 Level 1) ❏

- Do the children draw simple conclusions from their work? Do the children describe the different ways they have sorted objects, what is the same about objects in a set, how sets differ? (Ma1 Level 1) ❏

Number
Pupils count, order, add and subtract numbers when solving problems involving up to 10 objects. They read and write the numbers involved.

- Do the children count up to 10 objects? Do they estimate and check a number? Do they read and write numbers to 10? Do they order numbers to 10? (Ma2 Level 1) ❏

- Are the children beginning to use the fraction one half? (Ma2 Level 1) ❏

- Do the children understand addition as finding the total of two or more sets of objects? Do they understand subtraction as 'taking away' objects from a set and finding how many are left? (Ma2 Level 1) ❏

- Do the children add and subtract numbers of objects to 10? Are the children beginning to know some addition facts? (Ma2 Level 1) ❏

- Do the children solve addition/subtraction problems involving up to 10 objects? ❏

- Do they solve problems involving 1p or £1 coins? (Ma2 Level 1) ❏

- Do the children record their work with objects, pictures or diagrams? Are they beginning to use the symbols + and = to record additions? (Ma2 Level 1) ❏

Andrew Brodie: Solving Maths Problems 7–9 © A&C Black 2010

Shape, space and measures

When working with 2-D and 3-D shapes, pupils use everyday language to describe properties and positions. They measure and order objects using direct comparison and order events.

- Do the children use everyday language to describe properties of 2-D and 3-D shapes? Do they sort shapes and say how they have selected them? Do they use properties such as large, small, triangles, roll, stack? Are they beginning to refer to some features of shapes such as side and corner? Are they beginning to name the shapes they use in the context of an activity? (Ma3 Level 1) ❏

- Do the children use everyday language to describe positions of 2-D and 3-D shapes? Do they respond to and use positional language, eg 'behind', 'under', 'on top of', 'next to', 'in between'? Do they respond to and use directional language in talk about objects and movement, eg 'forwards', 'backwards', 'turn'? (Ma3 Level 1) ❏

- Do the children measure and order objects using direct comparison? Do they order everyday events and describe the sequence? Do they use the vocabulary of time including days of the week? Do they read the time on an analogue clock at the hour and begin to know the half hour? (Ma3 Level 1) ❏

Handling data

Pupils sort objects and classify them, demonstrating the criterion they have used.

- Do the children sort and classify objects? Do they sort using one criterion or sort into disjoint sets using two simple criteria such as thick/thin? Do they sort objects again using a different criterion? Do they sort into a given large scale Venn or Carroll diagram? Do they represent their work by using the objects they have sorted as a record or using objects/pictures to create simple block graphs? (Ma4 Level 1) ❏

- Do they demonstrate the criterion they have used? Do they respond to questions about how they have sorted objects and why each object belongs in a set? Do they talk about which set has most? Do they talk about how they have represented their work? (Ma4 Level 1) ❏

Guidelines for assessing mathematics
Level 2

Using and applying mathematics

Pupils select the mathematics they use in some classroom activities. They discuss their work using some mathematical language and are beginning to represent it using symbols and simple diagrams. They explain why an answer is correct.

- Do the children select the mathematics they use in some classroom activities, eg with support? Do they find a starting point, identifying key facts/relevant information? Do they use apparatus, diagrams, role-play, etc. to represent and clarify a problem? Do they move between different representations of a problem, eg a situation described in words, a diagram, etc. Do they adopt a suggested model or systematic approach? Do they make connections and apply their knowledge to similar situations? Do they use mathematical content from levels 1 and 2 to solve problems and investigate? (Ma1 Level 2) ❑

- Do the children discuss their work using mathematical language, eg with support? Do they describe the strategies and methods they use in their work? Do they engage with others' explanations, compare, evaluate? Are they beginning to represent their work using symbols and simple diagrams, eg with support? Do they use pictures, diagrams and symbols to communicate their thinking, or demonstrate a solution or process? Are they beginning to appreciate the need to record and develop their own methods of recording? (Ma1 Level 2) ❑

- Can the children explain why an answer is correct, eg with support? Can they predict what comes next in a simple number, shape or spatial pattern or sequence and give reasons for their opinion? (Ma1 Level 2) ❑

Number

Pupils count sets of objects reliably, and use mental recall of addition and subtraction facts to 10. They begin to understand the place value of each digit in a number and use this to order numbers up to 100. They choose the appropriate operation when solving addition and subtraction problems. They use the knowledge that subtraction is the inverse of addition. They use mental calculation strategies to solve number problems involving money and measures. They recognise sequences of numbers, including odd and even numbers.

- Do the children count sets of objects reliably, eg group objects in tens, twos or fives to count them? Are they beginning to understand the place value of each digit, using this to order numbers up to 100? Do they recognise sequences of numbers, including odd and even numbers, eg continue a sequence that increases or decreases in regular steps, recognise numbers from counting in tens or twos? (Ma2 Level 2) ❑

- Are the children beginning to use halves and quarters, eg in a practical context? Can they work out halves of numbers up to 20 and are they beginning to recall these? Can they relate the concept of half of a small quantity to the concept of half of a shape, eg shade one half or one quarter of a given shape? (Ma2 Level 2) ❑

- Do the children use the knowledge that subtraction is the inverse of addition, eg are they beginning to understand subtraction as 'difference'? Can they make related number sentences involving addition and subtraction? Do they understand halving as a way of 'undoing' doubling and vice versa? (Ma2 Level 2) ❑

- Do the children use mental recall of addition facts to 10, eg use place value to derive 30 + 70 = 100 from the known fact 3 + 7 = 10? Do they use mental calculation strategies to solve number problems including those involving money and measures? (Ma2 Level 2) ❑

Andrew Brodie: Solving Maths Problems 7–9 © A&C Black 2010

- Do the children choose the appropriate operation when solving addition and subtraction problems? Do they use repeated addition to solve multiplication problems? Are they beginning to use repeated subtraction or sharing equally to solve division problems? Can they solve number problems involving money and measures? (Ma2 Level 2)

- Do they record their work in writing, eg record their mental calculations as number sentences? (Ma2 Level 2)

Shape, space and measures

Pupils use mathematical names for common 3-D and 2-D shapes and describe their properties, including numbers of sides and corners. They distinguish between straight and turning movements, understand angles as a measure of turn, and recognise right angles in turns. They begin to use everyday non-standard and standard units to measure length and mass.

- Do the children use mathematical names for common 3-D and 2-D shapes, eg square, triangle, hexagon, pentagon, octagon, cube, cylinder, sphere, cuboid, pyramid? Do they describe their properties, including numbers of sides and corners? Do they make and talk about shapes referring to features and properties using language such as edge, face, corner? Do they sort 2-D and 3-D shapes according to a single criterion? Can they visualise frequently used 2-D and 3-D shapes? Are they beginning to understand the difference between shapes with two dimension and those with three? Do they recognise the properties that are the same even when a shape is enlarged? (Ma3 Level 2)

- Can the children describe the position of objects, eg by using ordinal numbers (first, second, third, …)? Do they recognise that a shape stays the same even when it is held up in different orientations? Can they distinguish between straight and turning movements, eg between left and right and between clockwise and anticlockwise? Do they recognise right angles in turns? (Ma3 Level 2)

- Do the children understand angle as a measure of turn, making whole turns, half turns and quarter turns? Are they beginning to use everyday non-standard and standard units to measure length and mass? Do they understand that numbers can be used to describe continuous measures? Do they know which measuring tools to use? Are they beginning to use a wider range of measures, eg a right angle checker or a time line? (Ma3 Level 2)

Handling data

Pupils sort objects and classify them using more than one criterion. When they have gathered information, pupils record results in simple lists, tables and block graphs, in order to communicate their findings.

- Do the children sort objects and classify them using more than one criterion, eg sort a set of shapes using two criteria such as triangle/not triangle and blue/not blue? Do they understand the vocabulary related to handling data, such as 'sort', 'group', 'set', 'list', 'table', 'most common', 'most popular'? Can they collect and sort data to test a simple hypothesis? Can they record results in simple lists, tables, pictograms and block graphs? (Ma4 Level 2)

- Can the children communicate their findings, using the simple lists, tables, pictograms and block graphs they have recorded, eg by responding to questions about the data they have presented and posing similar questions for others to answer? (Ma4 Level 2)

Guidelines for assessing mathematics
Level 3

Using and applying mathematics
Pupils try different approaches and find ways of overcoming difficulties that arise when they are solving problems. They are beginning to organise their work and check results. Pupils discuss their mathematical work and are beginning to explain their thinking. They use and interpret mathematical symbols and diagrams. Pupils show that they understand a general statement by finding particular examples that match it.

- Do the children select the mathematics they use in a wider range of classroom activities? For example: Do they use classroom discussions to break into a problem, recognising similarities to previous work? Do they put the problem into their own words? Do they use mathematical content from levels 2 and 3? Do they choose their own equipment appropriate to the task, including calculators? Do they try different approaches and find ways of overcoming difficulties that arise when they are solving problems? For example: Do they check their work and make appropriate corrections? Are they beginning to look for patterns in results as they work and do they use these to find other possible outcomes? (Ma1 Level 3)

- Are the children beginning to organise their work and check results? For example: Are they beginning to develop their own ways of recording? Do they develop an organised approach as they get into recording their work on a problem? Do they discuss their mathematical work and begin to explain their thinking? Do they use appropriate mathematical vocabulary? Do they talk about their findings by referring to their written work? Do they use and interpret mathematical symbols and diagrams? (Ma1 Level 3)

- Do the children understand a general statement by finding particular examples that match it? For example: Can they make a generalisation, with the assistance of probing questions and prompts? Do they review their work and reasoning? For example: Do they respond to 'What if?' questions? When they have solved a problem, can they pose a similar problem for a partner? (Ma1 Level 3)

Number
Pupils show understanding of place value in numbers up to 1000 and use this to make approximations. They begin to use decimal notation and to recognise negative numbers, in contexts such as money and temperature. Pupils use mental recall of addition and subtraction facts to 20 in solving problems involving larger numbers. They add and subtract numbers with two digits mentally and numbers with three digits using written methods. They use mental recall of the 2, 3, 4, 5 and 10 multiplication tables and derive the associated division facts. They solve whole number problems involving multiplication or division, including those that give rise to remainders. They use simple fractions that are several parts of a whole and recognise when two simple fractions are equivalent.

- Do the children understand place value in numbers to 1000? For example: Do they represent/compare numbers using number lines, 100 squares, base 10 materials, etc? Do they recognise that some numbers can be represented as different arrays? Do they use understanding of place value to multiply/divide whole numbers by 10 (whole number answers)? Can the children use place value to make approximations? Do they recognise negative numbers in contexts such as temperature? Do they recognise a wider range of sequences, eg recognise sequences of multiples of 2, 5 and 10? (Ma2 Level 3)

- Do the children use simple fractions that are several parts of a whole and recognise when two simple fractions are equivalent? Do they understand and use unit fractions such as $\frac{1}{2}, \frac{1}{4}, \frac{1}{3}, \frac{1}{5}, \frac{1}{10}$ and find those fractions of shapes and sets of objects? Do they recognise and record fractions that are several parts of the whole, such as $\frac{3}{4}, \frac{2}{5}$? Do they recognise some fractions that are equivalent to $\frac{1}{2}$? Are they beginning to use decimal notation in contexts such as money? For example: Can they order decimals with one decimal place or two decimal places in the context of money? Do they know that £3.06 equals 306p? (Ma2 Level 3)

- Can the children derive associated division facts from known multiplication facts? Do they use inverses to find missing whole numbers in problems such as 'I think of a number, double it and add 5. The answer is 35. What was my number?'? Are the children beginning to understand the role of the equals sign? For example: Can they solve 'balancing' problems such as 7 x 10 = 82 – a/w answer box? (Ma2 Level 3)

Andrew Brodie: Solving Maths Problems 7-9 © A&C Black 2010

- Can the children add and subtract two-digit numbers mentally? Can they use mental recall of the 2, 3, 4, 5 and 10 multiplication tables? Are they beginning to know multiplication facts for the 6, 7, 8 and 9 multiplication tables? (Ma2 Level 3) ❏

- Can the children use mental recall of addition and subtraction facts to 20 in solving problems involving larger numbers? Do they solve whole number problems including those involving multiplication or division that may give rise to remainders? (Ma2 Level 3) ❏

- Can the children add and subtract three-digit numbers using a written method? Can they multiply and divide two-digit numbers by 2, 3, 4, 5 or 10 with whole number answers and remainders? (Ma2 Level 3) ❏

Shape, space and measures

Pupils classify 3-D and 2-D shapes in various ways using mathematical properties such as reflective symmetry for 2-D shapes. They use non-standard units, standard metric units of length, capacity and mass, and standard units of time, in a range of contexts.

- Can the children classify 3-D and 2-D shapes in various ways using mathematical properties such as reflective symmetry for 2-D shapes? Do they sort objects and shapes using more than one criterion? Are they beginning to understand the terms regular and irregular? Do they recognise right angles in shapes in different orientations? Do they recognise angles that are bigger or smaller than 90º? Are they beginning to use the terms acute and obtuse? Do they recognise right-angled and equilateral triangles? Can they demonstrate that a shape has reflectional symmetry by folding? Do they recognise when a shape does not have a line of symmetry? Can they recognise common 3-D shapes? Can they relate 3-D shapes to drawings and photographs of them? Are they beginning to recognise nets of familiar 3-D shapes? (Ma3 Level 3) ❏

- Do the children recognise shapes in different orientations? Can they reflect shapes, presented on a grid, in a vertical or horizontal mirror line? Are they beginning to reflect simple shapes in a mirror line presented at 45º? Can they describe position and movement using terms such as left/right, clockwise/ anticlockwise, quarter turn/90º? (Ma3 Level 3) ❏

- Do the children use non-standard units and standard metric units of length, capacity and mass in a range of contexts? For example: Can they measure a length to the nearest ½ cm? Can they read simple scales? Do they use standard units of time? Can they read a 12-hour clock and calculate time durations that do not go over the hour? Do they use a wider range of measures? For example: Are they beginning to understand area as a measure of surface and perimeter as a measure of length? Are they beginning to find areas of shapes by counting squares? Do they recognise angles as a measure of turn and know that one whole turn is 360 degrees? (Ma3 Level 3) ❏

Handling data

Pupils extract and interpret information presented in simple tables and lists. They construct bar charts and pictograms, where the symbol represents a group of units, to communicate information they have gathered, and the interpret information presented in these forms.

- Can the children gather information by deciding what data to collect to answer a question and making appropriate choices for recording information? Can they construct bar charts and pictograms, where the symbol represents a group of units? Do they decide how best to present data, eg whether a bar chart, a pictogram or a Venn diagram would show the information most clearly? Can they decide upon an appropriate scale for a graph? Do they use Venn and Carroll diagrams to record their sorting and classifying of information? (Ma4 Level 3) ❏

- Can the children extract and interpret information presented in simple tables, lists, bar charts or pictograms? Can they use a key to interpret data? Can they read scales labelled in twos, fives and tens, including reading between labelled divisions? Can they compare data? Can they respond to questions of a more complex nature such as 'How many children took part in this survey altogether?'? Can they understand the idea of certain and impossible relating to probability in the context of data regarding everyday situations? (Ma4 Level 3) ❏

Amy's money

Teacher's notes

Sheets 1-4 to be used together.

Suggested objective: *Use mental calculation strategies to solve number problems involving money.*

Problems: *Make comparisons between the amounts of money each child has.*
Who has the most? Who has the least?   Who has more than 50p? Who has less than 50p? How much more money does each person need to have £1?

Andrew Brodie: Solving Maths Problems 7–9 © A&C Black 2010

Name _____ Date _____

Millie's money

Teacher's notes

Sheets 1-4 to be used together.
Suggested objective: *Use mental calculation strategies to solve number problems involving money.*

Problems: *Make comparisons between the amounts of money each child has.*
Who has the most? Who has the least?   Who has more than 50p? Who has less than 50p? How much more money does each person need to have £1?

Jack's money

Teacher's notes

Sheets 1-4 to be used together.
Suggested objective: *Use mental calculation strategies to solve number problems involving money.*

Problems: *Make comparisons between the amounts of money each child has.*
Who has the most? Who has the least?   Who has more than 50p? Who has less than 50p? How much more money does each person need to have £1?

Ed's money

Teacher's notes

Sheets 1-4 to be used together.

Suggested objective: *Use mental calculation strategies to solve number problems involving money.*

Problems: *Make comparisons between the amounts of money each child has.*
Who has the most? Who has the least? Who has more than 50p? Who has less than 50p? How much more money does each person need to have £1?

Andrew Brodie: Solving Maths Problems 7–9 © A&C Black 2010

How much money?

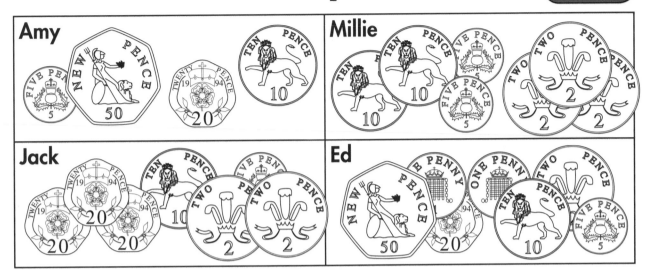

How much money has Amy got?

How much money has Millie got?

How much money has Jack got?

How much money has Ed got?

How much more money would Ed need to have £5?

If Amy had double her amount of money, how much would she have?

If Millie spends half her money, how much would she have?

If the children all put their money together, how much would there be?

How much more would they need to make the total amount £5?

Teacher's notes

Suggested objective: *Use mental calculation strategies to solve number problems involving money.*

Problems: Children answer the questions above. Are they beginning to look for patterns in results as they work and do they use these to find other possible outcomes? Do they understand halving as a way of undoing, doubling and vice versa?

Andrew Brodie: Solving Maths Problems 7–9 © A&C Black 2010

Name _____ Date _____

How many ways can you make 20p?

Here are the types of coins you can use:

1p

2p

5p

10p

20p

How many ways can you make 20p? Some ways are shown for you. How many other ways can you find?

20p	1 x 20p	**20p**	
20p	2 x 10p	**20p**	
20p	1 x 10p, 2 x 5p	**20p**	
20p		**20p**	
20p		**20p**	
20p		**20p**	
20p		**20p**	
20p		**20p**	
20p		**20p**	
20p		**20p**	

Teacher's notes

Suggested objective: *Devise a strategy for finding all ways of making a total of 20p.*

Problem: *How many ways can you make 20p?*
Ask individual children to make 20p, using different coins. There are only nineteen ways of making 20p. Do the children work methodically? Do they make and use lists and tables to organise and interpret their information? Do they identify patterns?

Discussion sheet: How many connections can you make?

Sheet 7

Look: 5 + 4 = 9

We can use this fact to find other calculation sentences.

Here are some examples:

$$9 - 4 = 5$$

$$50 + 40 = 90$$

$$500 + 400 = 900$$

Can you find any others?

Teacher's notes

Suggested objective: *Use patterns to find other outcomes.*

Problem: *How many connections can you make?*
This sheet is designed to form an introduction to a set of activities featuring connections between calculations. Are the children looking for patterns in results? Do they use these to find other results? Do they understand place value in numbers to 1000? Can they use mental recall of addition and subtraction facts to 20 in solving problems involving larger numbers?

How many connections can you make?

Look: 5 + 2 = 7

We can use this fact to find other calculation sentences.

Here are some examples:

7 – 2 = 5

50 + 20 = 70

500 + 200 = 700

Find some connected calculations for each of those given here.

6 + 2 = 8
_____
_____
_____
_____
_____
_____

4 + 2 = 6
_____
_____
_____
_____
_____
_____

3 + 4 = 7
_____
_____
_____
_____
_____
_____

Teacher's notes

Suggested objective: *Use patterns to find other outcomes.*

Problem: *How many connections can you make?*
Are the children looking for patterns in results? Do they use these to find other results? Do they understand place value in numbers to 1000? Can they use mental recall of addition and subtraction facts to 20 in solving problems involving larger numbers?

How many connections can you make?

Look: 9 – 3 = 6

We can use this fact to find other calculation sentences.

Here are some examples:

9 – 6 = 3

6 + 3 = 9

60 + 30 = 90

Find some connected calculations for each of those given here.

10 – 7 = 3	10 – 4 = 6	10 – 2 = 8
_____	_____	_____
_____	_____	_____
_____	_____	_____
_____	_____	_____

Teacher's notes

Suggested objective: *Use patterns to find other outcomes.*

Problem: *How many connections can you make?*
Are the children looking for patterns in results? Do they use these to find other results? Do they understand place value in numbers to 1000? Can they use mental recall of addition and subtraction facts to 20 in solving problems involving larger numbers?

How many connections can you make?

$$8 - 5 = 3$$

We can use this fact to find other calculation sentences.

Here are some examples:

$$8 - 3 = 5$$

$$5 + 3 = 8$$

$$50 + 30 = 80$$

Find some connected calculations for each of those given here.

$7 - 5 = 2$	$6 - 4 = 2$	$9 - 2 = 7$

Teacher's notes

Suggested objective: *Use patterns to find other outcomes.*

Problem: *How many connections can you make?*
Are the children looking for patterns in results? Do they use these to find other results? Do they understand place value in numbers to 1000? Can they use mental recall of addition and subtraction facts to 20 in solving problems involving larger numbers?

Andrew Brodie: Solving Maths Problems 7-9 © A&C Black 2010

How many connections can you make?

$$12 + 3 = 15$$

We can use this fact to find other calculation sentences.

Here are some examples:

$$15 - 3 = 12$$

$$120 + 30 = 150$$

$$150 - 120 = 30$$

Find some connected calculations for each of those given here.

$16 + 4 = 20$
_____
_____
_____
_____
_____

$15 + 2 = 17$
_____
_____
_____
_____
_____

$13 + 3 = 16$
_____
_____
_____
_____
_____

Teacher's notes

Suggested objective: *Use patterns to find other outcomes.*

Problem: *How many connections can you make?*
Are the children looking for patterns in results? Do they use these to find other results? Do they understand place value in numbers to 1000? (Note that this sheet can lead to the use of numbers beyond 100.) Can they use mental recall of addition and subtraction facts to 20 in solving problems involving larger numbers?

Andrew Brodie: Solving Maths Problems 7-9 © A&C Black 2010

Can you solve balance problems?

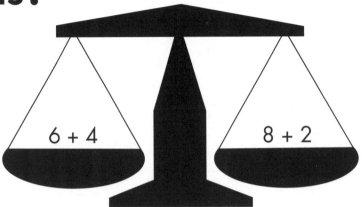

The scales are balanced because both calculations have the same answer.

Find the missing number to write in each box. Remember, both sides of the equals sign (=) must balance.

10 + 4 = 8 + ☐

6 + 8 = 10 + ☐

11 + 6 = ☐ + 9

12 + ☐ = 16 + 4

8 + ☐ = 9 + 4

12 + 5 = 13 + ☐

13 + 6 = ☐ + 5

8 + 4 = ☐ + 3

☐ + 15 = 30 – 6

☐ + 10 = 15 + 6

Teacher's notes

Suggested objective: *Solve 'balancing' problems.*

Problem: *Can you make both sides of the equals sign balance?*
Are the children beginning to understand the role of the equals sign? Many children assume that the equals sign leads to an 'answer' but they will find much of their later maths work much easier if they understand that the equals sign indicates a balance of values. Help them to see that each of these 'balancing problems' can be solved by finding the value of one side, then making the other side worth the same.

Andrew Brodie: Solving Maths Problems 7–9 © A&C Black 2010

Can you solve balance problems?

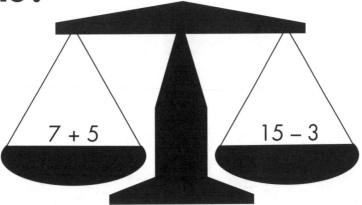

The scales are balanced because both calculations have the same answer.

Find the missing number to write in each box. Remember, both sides of the equals sign (=) must balance.

6 + 4 = 8 + ☐

10 − 2 = 14 − ☐

20 + 5 = ☐ + 15

2 + ☐ = 12 − 4

8 + ☐ = 6 + 6

☐ + 9 = 20 − 4

7 + 5 = 3 + ☐

14 + 6 = ☐ + 2

16 + 8 = ☐ + 20

7 + ☐ = 20 − 7

☐ + 3 = 15 − 9

☐ + 10 = 22 − 4

Andrew Brodie: Solving Maths Problems 7–9 © A&C Black 2010

Can you solve balance problems?

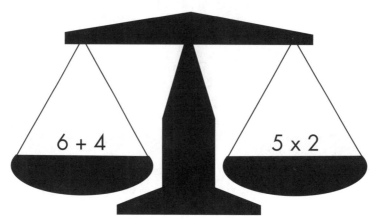

The scales are balanced because both calculations have the same answer.

Find the missing number to write in each box. Remember, both sides of the equals sign (=) must balance.

10 + 4 = 7 x ☐

16 + 5 = 7 x ☐

12 + 6 = ☐ x 9

12 + ☐ = 4 x 4

8 + ☐ = 6 x 2

☐ + 10 = 6 x 4

12 + 8 = 5 x ☐

13 + 2 = ☐ x 5

20 + 5 = ☐ x 5

10 + ☐ = 6 x 3

☐ + 5 = 9 x 2

☐ + 12 = 8 x 4

Teacher's notes

Suggested objective: *Solve 'balancing' problems.*

Problem: *Can you make both sides of the equals sign balance?*
Help the children to see that each of these 'balancing problems' can be solved by finding the value of one side, then making the other side worth the same.

Andrew Brodie: Solving Maths Problems 7–9 © A&C Black 2010

Can you solve balance problems?

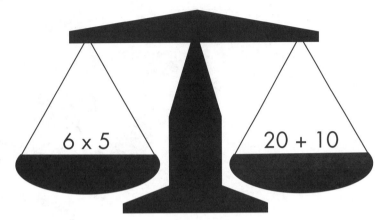

The scales are balanced because both calculations have the same answer.

Find the missing number to write in each box. Remember, both sides of the equals sign (=) must balance.

20 – 8 = 6 x [   ]

9 x 4 = 20 + [   ]

9 x 3 = [   ] + 22

9 x [   ] = 25 + 2

8 x [   ] = 30 + 2

[   ] x 2 = 30 – 12

24 + 6 = 5 x [   ]

7 x 4 = [   ] – 2

8 x 5 = [   ] – 10

10 x [   ] = 60 – 10

[   ] x 2 = 20 – 8

[   ] x 3 = 30 – 9

Teacher's notes

Suggested objective: *Solve 'balancing' problems.*

Problem: *Can you make both sides of the equals sign balance?*
Help the children to see that each of these 'balancing problems' can be solved by finding the value of one side, then making the other side worth the same.

Andrew Brodie: Solving Maths Problems 7–9 © A&C Black 2010

Can you hit the target?

Find an addition, a subtraction, a multiplication and a division for each of the target numbers. Write your calculations in the arrows.

$30 \div 2$ $11 + 4$ **15** $20 - 5$ 5×3

12

10

20

25

Teacher's notes

Suggested objective: *Use all four rules of number.*

Problem: *Can you create calculations using addition, subtraction, multiplication and division?*

Note that this activity gives similar practice to that provided by the 'balancing' problems.

Do the children try different approaches and find ways of overcoming difficulties that arise when they are solving problems? For example: Do they check their work and make appropriate corrections? Are they beginning to look for patterns in results as they work and do they use these to find other possible outcomes?

Andrew Brodie: Solving Maths Problems 7–9 © A&C Black 2010

Discussion sheet:
What number am I thinking of?

> I think of a number.
> I add 3. The answer is 10.
> What number did I
> first think of?

Teacher's notes

Suggested objective: *Use inverses to find missing numbers in word problems.*

Problem: *What number am I thinking of?*

This sheet is designed to form an introduction to a set of activities in which the pupils have to use inverse calculations to find missing numbers. This is an extremely difficult concept for many children. The sheets here involve one-step problem-solving whereas later sheets involve two steps.

Are the children looking for patterns in results? Do they use these to find other results? Can the children derive associated division facts from known multiplication facts? Can the children use mental recall of addition and subtraction facts to 20 in solving problems involving larger numbers?

What number am I thinking of?

I think of a number.
I add 7.
The answer is 19.

What number did
I first think of?

I think of a number.
I add 6.
The answer is 14.

What number did
I first think of?

I think of a number.
I add 8.
The answer is 17.

What number did
I first think of?

I think of a number.
I add 10.
The answer is 22.

What number did
I first think of?

Teacher's notes

Suggested objective: *Use inverses to find missing numbers in word problems.*

Problem: *What number am I thinking of?*

Are the children looking for patterns in results? Do they use these to find other results? Can the children use mental recall of addition and subtraction facts to 20 in solving problems involving larger numbers? Do the children use the knowledge that subtraction is the inverse of addition? Many children will find this concept quite difficult but those who are confident could make up some of their own problems like the ones on the sheet. They could share these with other confident children.

What number am I thinking of?

I think of a number.
I subtract 3.
The answer is 8.

What number did
I first think of?

I think of a number.
I subtract 7.
The answer is 9.

What number did
I first think of?

I think of a number.
I subtract 5.
The answer is 7.

What number did
I first think of?

I think of a number.
I subtract 6.
The answer is 8.

What number did
I first think of?

Teacher's notes

Suggested objective: *Use inverses to find missing numbers in word problems.*

Problem: *What number am I thinking of?*
Are the children looking for patterns in results? Do they use these to find other results? Can the children use mental recall of addition and subtraction facts to 20 in solving problems involving larger numbers? Do the children use the knowledge that subtraction is the inverse of addition? Many children will find this concept quite difficult but those who are confident could make up some of their own problems like the ones on the sheet. They could share these with other confident children.

Name _____ Date _____

What number am I thinking of?

I think of a number.
I multiply by 2.
The answer is 16.

What number did
I first think of?

I think of a number.
I multiply by 3.
The answer is 27.

What number did
I first think of?

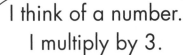

I think of a number.
I multiply by 4.
The answer is 24.

What number did
I first think of?

I think of a number.
I multiply by 5.
The answer is 45.

What number did
I first think of?

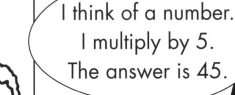

Teacher's notes

Suggested objective: *Use inverses to find missing numbers in word problems.*

Problem: *What number am I thinking of?*
Are the children looking for patterns in results? Do they use these to find other results? Can the children derive associated division facts from known multiplication facts? Many children will find this concept quite difficult but those who are confident could make up some of their own problems like the ones on the sheet. They could share these with other confident children.

Name _____ Date _____

What number am I thinking of?

I think of a number.
I divide by 2.
The answer is 7.

What number did
I first think of?

[ ]

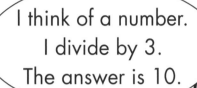

I think of a number.
I divide by 3.
The answer is 10.

What number did
I first think of?

[ ]

I think of a number.
I divide by 4.
The answer is 8.

What number did
I first think of?

[ ]

I think of a number.
I divide by 5.
The answer is 6.

What number did
I first think of?

[ ]

Teacher's notes

Suggested objective: *Use inverses to find missing numbers in word problems.*

Problem: *What number am I thinking of?*
Are the children looking for patterns in results? Do they use these to find other results? Can the children derive associated division facts from known multiplication facts? Many children will find this concept quite difficult but those who are confident could make up some of their own problems like the ones on the sheet. They could share these with other confident children.

Discussion sheet: Which is the best value?

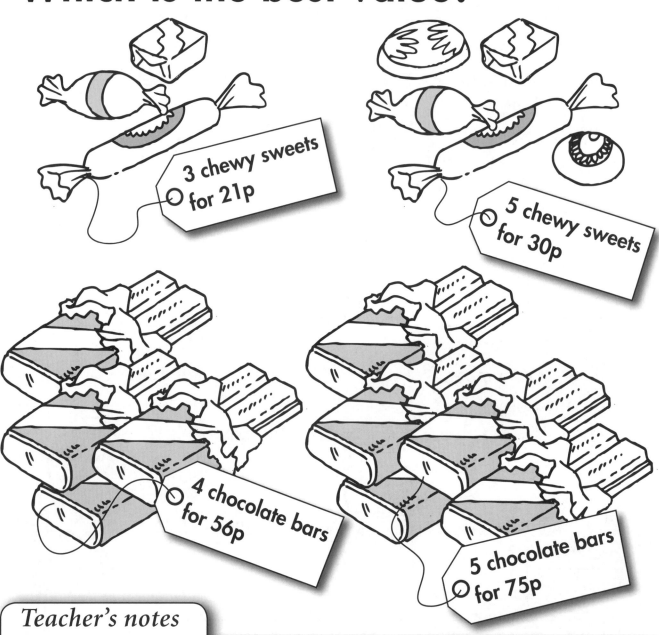

3 chewy sweets for 21p

5 chewy sweets for 30p

4 chocolate bars for 56p

5 chocolate bars for 75p

Teacher's notes

Suggested objective: *Developing an organised approach to solving a problem.*

Problem: *Which is the best value for money?*

This sheet is designed to form an introduction to a set of activities in which the pupils have to find best value for money. The idea of finding best value may be familiar to the pupils from everyday shopping activities but ask them *how* they can carry out the process. Some pupils may be able to state that finding the cost of one item from each set will allow a comparison to be made. You could provide the children with coins to investigate the solutions.

Note that in the second example the best value is provided by the set of 4 rather than the set of 5. You could explain that in normal shopping situations the larger set will often be the best value but that this is not always the case.

Which is the best value?

Gina bought 4 lollipops for 36p.

Sam bought 6 lollipops for 48p.

Who had the best value for money?

Show how you
worked this out.

Teacher's notes

Suggested objective: *Developing an organised approach to solving a problem.*

Problem: *Which are the best value?*
The idea of finding best value may be familiar to the pupils from everyday shopping activities but ask them how they can carry out the process. Some pupils may be able to state that finding the cost of one item from each set will allow a comparison to be made. You could encourage the children to use coins to investigate the solutions. Support the children in recording their findings – they could draw coins to show the value of each lollipop.

Name _____ Date _____

What change will I have?

Skipping rope 65p

Ball 62p

Cupcake 30p

Beanbag 45p

Bubble mix 36p

Book 50p

Bag of marbles 25p

Find the change from £1 if you bought:

A bag of marbles.	Change from £1 =	
A beanbag.	Change from £1 =	
A skipping rope.	Change from £1 =	
A ball.	Change from £1 =	
A cupcake.	Change from £1 =	
A book.	Change from £1 =	
A Bubble mix.	Change from £1 =	

Teacher's notes

Suggested objective: *Use mental calculation strategies to solve number problems involving money.*

Problem: *What change will I have?*
This is the first sheet of money activities centred around a school fair. The children need to interpret the wording of the questions then to use their knowledge of addition and subtraction facts to find the answers.

Name _____ Date _____

What could I buy?

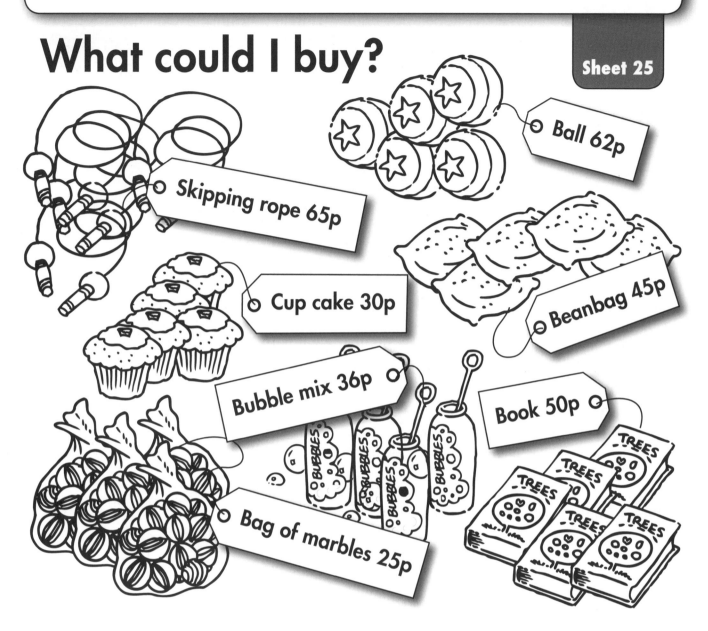

Ball 62p

Skipping rope 65p

Cup cake 30p

Beanbag 45p

Bubble mix 36p

Book 50p

Bag of marbles 25p

I want to buy two items. I have only got £1 to spend. What could I buy?

_____

_____

Teacher's notes

Suggested objective: *Use mental calculation strategies to solve number problems involving money.*

Problem: *What could I buy with £1?*
The children need to interpret the wording of the question then to use their knowledge of addition and subtraction facts to find all the possible answers. Encourage them to notice that there are several ways to solve the problem – they could, for example, buy two bags of marbles, a bag of marbles and a beanbag, a beanbag and a book, etc. How many different combinations can they find?
Extension problem: *Find the change from £1 for each combination.*

Andrew Brodie: Solving Maths Problems 7–9 © A&C Black 2010

How many cupcakes could I buy?

Cupcakes 30p each

How many cupcakes could I buy if I had £3?

answer:

How many cupcakes could I buy if I had £2?

answer:

How much more money would I need to buy one more cupcake?

answer:

Teacher's notes

Suggested objective: *Use mental calculation strategies to solve number problems involving money.*

Problem: *How many cup cakes could I buy?*
The children need to interpret the wording of the question then to use their knowledge of addition and multiplication facts to find all the possible answers. They can use the larger space to show their working out. Encourage them to notice that they don't need the complete 30 pence to buy one more cup cake if they have £2 to spend.

How many books could I buy?

Books 50p each

Each book costs 50p.

How many books could I buy for 50p?

How many books could I buy for £1?

How many books could I buy for £1.50?

How many books could I buy for £2?

How many books could I buy for £2.50?

How many books could I buy for £3?

Can you see a pattern in your answers?

Use the pattern to help you to answer these questions:

How many books could I buy for £3.50?

How many books could I buy for £4?

How many books could I buy for £4.50?

How many books could I buy for £5?

Teacher's notes

Suggested objective: *Look for patterns in results and use these to find other results.*

Problem: *How many books could I buy?*
The children need to interpret the wording of the question then to use their knowledge of addition and multiplication facts to find all the possible answers. Talk about the pattern of the answers with them. How far can they continue the pattern? More able pupils may be able to use the answers to derive the 50 times table!

How many bags of marbles could I buy?

Bag of marbles 25p

Each bag of marbles costs 25p.

How many bags of marbles could I buy for 50p?

How many bags of marbles could I buy for £1?

How many bags of marbles could I buy for £1.50?

How many bags of marbles could I buy for £2?

How many bags of marbles could I buy for £2.50?

How many bags of marbles could I buy for £3?

Can you see a pattern in your answers? Use the pattern to help you to answer these questions:

How many bags of marbles could I buy for £3.50?

How many bags of marbles could I buy for £4?

How many bags of marbles could I buy for £4.50?

How many bags of marbles could I buy for £5?

Teacher's notes

Suggested objective: *Look for patterns in results and use these to find other results.*

Problem: *How many bags of marbles could I buy?*
The children need to interpret the wording of the question then to use their knowledge of addition and multiplication facts to find all the possible answers. Talk about the pattern of the answers with them. How far can they continue the pattern? More able pupils may be able to use the answers to derive the 25 times table, but note that there are obvious gaps in the answers that would need to be filled.

Andrew Brodie: Solving Maths Problems 7–9 © A&C Black 2010

What do three cost?

Ball 62p

Skipping rope 65p

Cupcake 30p

Beanbag 45p

Bubble mix 36p

Book 50p

Bag of marbles 25p

What do three bags of marbles cost altogether?

What do three beanbags cost altogether?

What do three skipping ropes cost altogether?

What do three balls cost altogether?

What do three cupcakes cost altogether?

What do three books cost altogether?

What do three lots of bubble mix cost altogether?

Teacher's notes

Suggested objective: *Use mental calculation strategies to solve number problems involving money.*

Problem: *What do three cost?*
The children need use their knowledge of addition and multiplication facts to find the answers. They could use coins to answer each question.

Andrew Brodie: Solving Maths Problems 7-9 © A&C Black 2010

Name _____ Date _____

What do four cost?

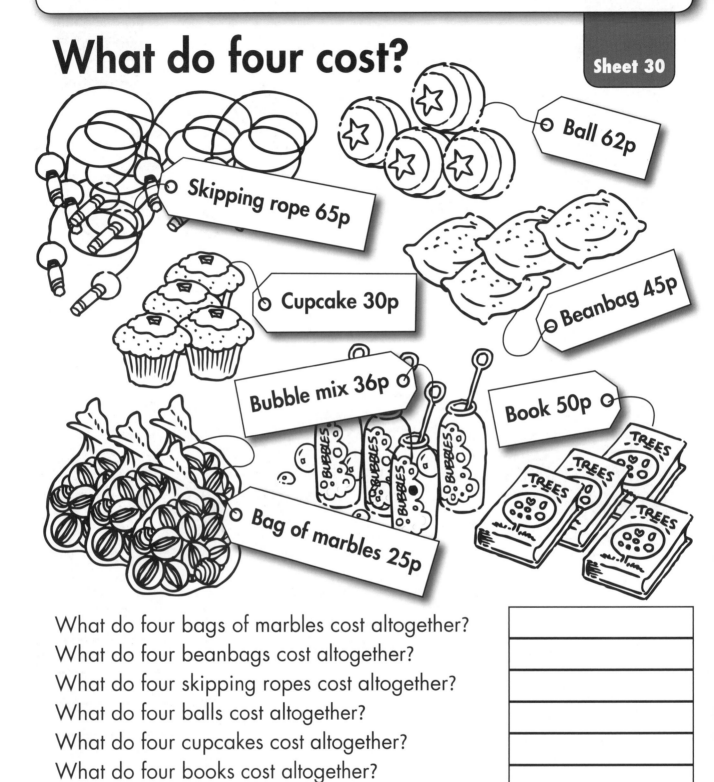

Ball 62p

Skipping rope 65p

Cupcake 30p

Beanbag 45p

Bubble mix 36p

Book 50p

Bag of marbles 25p

What do four bags of marbles cost altogether?

What do four beanbags cost altogether?

What do four skipping ropes cost altogether?

What do four balls cost altogether?

What do four cupcakes cost altogether?

What do four books cost altogether?

What do four lots of bubble mix cost altogether?

Teacher's notes

Suggested objective: *Use mental calculation strategies to solve number problems involving money.*

Problem: *What do four cost?*

The children need use their knowledge of addition and multiplication facts to find the answers. They could use coins to answer each question.

Andrew Brodie: Solving Maths Problems 7–9 © A&C Black 2010

What is the total cost?

Skipping rope 65p

Ball 62p

Cupcake 30p

Beanbag 45p

Bubble mix 36p

Book 50p

Bag of marbles 25p

If I buy one of each item at the school fair what would the total cost be?

answer:

What change would I have from a £5 note?

answer:

Can you find the pattern?

We can find two additions using whole numbers to make 1:

1 + 0 = 1   0 + 1 = 1

These are the additions using whole numbers to make 2:

2 + 0 = 2   0 + 2 = 2   1 + 1 = 2

These are the additions using pairs of whole numbers to make 3:

3 + 0 = 3   0 + 3 = 3   1 + 2 = 3   2 + 1 = 3

Find the additions to make **4**, using pairs of whole numbers:

_____

Find the additions to make **5**, using pairs of whole numbers :

_____

How many additions do you think you could find to make **6**, using pairs of whole numbers ?

_____

Teacher's notes

Suggested objective: *Look for patterns in results and use these to find other results.*

Problem: *Can you find the pattern?*
The children need to use their knowledge of addition facts to find all the possible answers. Talk about the pattern of the answers with them. Notice that the last question is different to the others – this is to encourage the children to investigate the pattern further.

Andrew Brodie: Solving Maths Problems 7–9 © A&C Black 2010

Can you find the pattern?

We can find two additions using whole numbers to make 1:

1 + 0 = 1   0 + 1 = 1

These are the additions using whole numbers to make 2:

2 + 0 = 2   0 + 2 = 2   1 + 1 = 2

These are the additions using pairs of whole numbers to make 3:

3 + 0 = 3   0 + 3 = 3   1 + 2 = 3   2 + 1 = 3

Find the additions to make **7**, using pairs of whole numbers:

_____

Find the additions to make **8**, using pairs of whole numbers:

_____

Find the additions to make **9**, using pairs of whole numbers :

_____

Teacher's notes

Suggested objective: *Look for patterns in results and use these to find other results.*

Problem: *Can you follow the pattern?*
The children need to use their knowledge of addition facts to find all the possible answers. Talk about the pattern of the answers with them.
Extension Problem: Ask how many additions could be found to make higher numbers such as 15, 16, 20, etc, using pairs of whole numbers.

Can you make the horse times table?

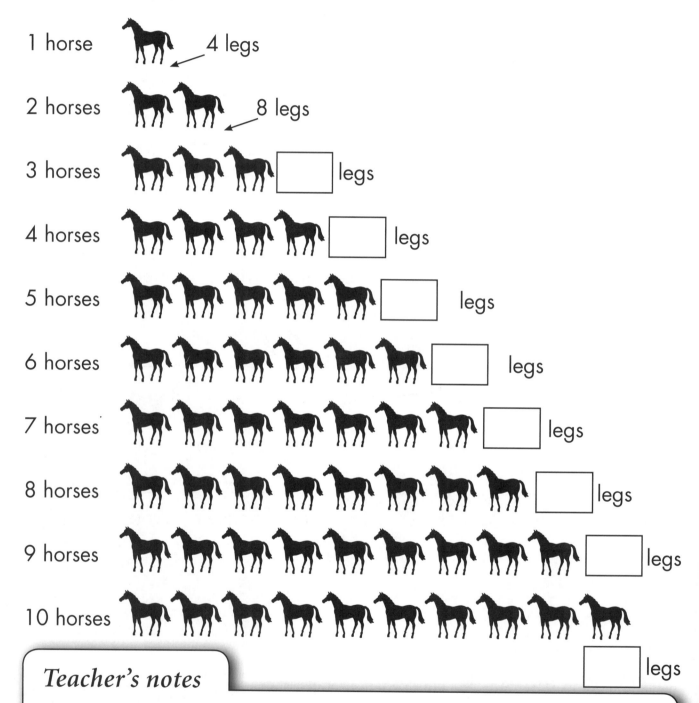

1 horse   4 legs

2 horses   8 legs

3 horses   ☐ legs

4 horses   ☐ legs

5 horses   ☐ legs

6 horses   ☐ legs

7 horses   ☐ legs

8 horses   ☐ legs

9 horses   ☐ legs

10 horses   ☐ legs

Teacher's notes

Suggested objective: *Look for patterns in results and use these to find other results.*

Problem: *Can you make the horse times table?*

This is, of course, the four times table derived from considering the total number of legs for each set of horses. The advantage of creating the table in this way is that the products can be related to real 'objects', i.e. the horses' legs. Many children find this an easier concept, particularly when they need to apply the results to further problems – these problems are on sheet 35.

Name _____ Date _____

Using the horse times table

Example:

What is the total number of legs that 13 horses have?

We know that 10 horses have 40 legs altogether and that 3 horses have 12 legs altogether:

40 legs

12 legs

40 + 12 = 52
So, 13 horses have 52 legs altogether.

What is the total number of legs that 15 horses have?

What is the total number of legs that 17 horses have?

What is the total number of legs that 12 horses have?

What is the total number of legs that 18 horses have?

What is the total number of legs that 20 horses have?

Teacher's notes

Suggested objective: *Look for patterns in results and use these to find other results.*

Problem: *Can you use the horse times table?*
The children can use the 'horse times table' that they completed on sheet 34 to help them to solve the problems. You could 'formalise' each question by writing it out as a number sentence after the children have found the answers. For example, you could show the children that the 13 horses question could be written out as 13 x 4 = 52. Ask the children to show working out on the back of this sheet.

Name _____ Date _____

Can you make the foot times table?

1 foot   ← 5 toes

2 feet   ← 10 toes

3 feet   [   ] toes

4 feet   [   ] toes

5 feet   [   ] toes

6 feet   [   ] toes

7 feet   [   ] toes

8 feet   [   ] toes

9 feet   [   ] toes

10 feet   [   ] toes

Teacher's notes

Suggested objective: *Look for patterns in results and use these to find other results.*

Problem: *Can you make the foot times table?*

This is, of course, the five times table derived from considering the total number of toes for each set of feet. The advantage of creating the table in this way is that the products can be related to real 'objects', i.e. the toes on the feet. Many children find this an easier concept, particularly when they need to apply the results to further problems – these problems are on sheet 37.

Andrew Brodie: Solving Maths Problems 7-9 © A&C Black 2010

Using the foot times table

Example:

What is the total number of toes that 14 feet have?

We know that 10 feet have 50 toes altogether and that 4 feet have 20 toes altogether:

50 toes

20 toes

50 + 20 = 70
So, 14 feet have 70 toes altogether.

What is the total number of toes that 19 feet have?

What is the total number of toes that 11 feet have?

What is the total number of toes that 17 feet have?

What is the total number of toes that 16 feet have?

What is the total number of toes that 20 feet have?

Teacher's notes

Suggested objective: *Look for patterns in results and use these to find other results.*

Problem: *Can you use the foot times table?*
The children can use the 'foot times table' that they completed on sheet 36 to help them to solve the problems. You may wish to 'formalise' each question by writing it out as a number sentence after the children have found the answers. For example, you could show the children that the 14 feet question could be written out as 14 x 5 = 70. Ask the children to show working out on the back of this sheet.

Can you make the ant times table?

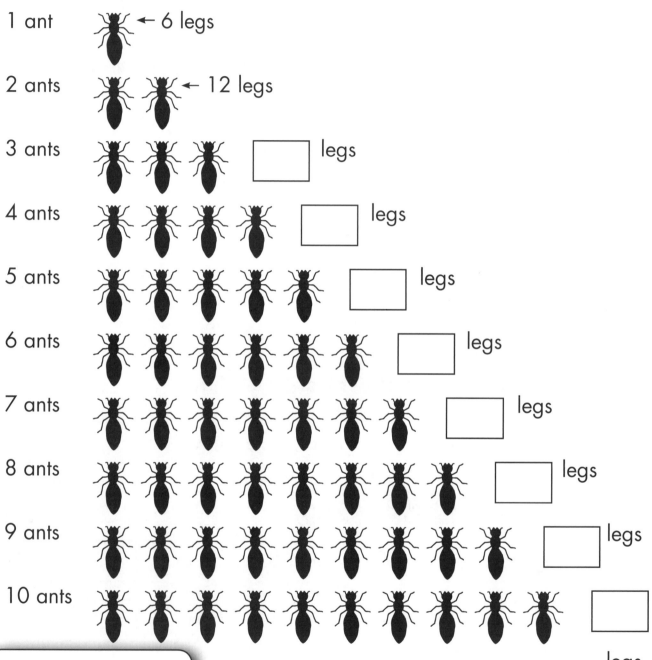

1 ant   ← 6 legs

2 ants   ← 12 legs

3 ants   [   ] legs

4 ants   [   ] legs

5 ants   [   ] legs

6 ants   [   ] legs

7 ants   [   ] legs

8 ants   [   ] legs

9 ants   [   ] legs

10 ants   [   ]
               legs

Teacher's notes

Suggested objective: *Look for patterns in results and use these to find other results.*

Problem: *Can you make the ant times table?*

This is, of course, the six times table derived from considering the total number of legs for each set of ants. The advantage of creating the table in this way is that the products can be related to real 'objects', i.e. the legs on the ants. Many children find this an easier concept, particularly when they need to apply the results to further problems – these problems are on sheet 39.

Andrew Brodie: Solving Maths Problems 7–9 © A&C Black 2010

Name _____ Date _____

Using the ant times table

Example:

What is the total number of legs that 17 ants have?

We know that 10 ants have 60 legs altogether and that 7 ants have 42 legs altogether:

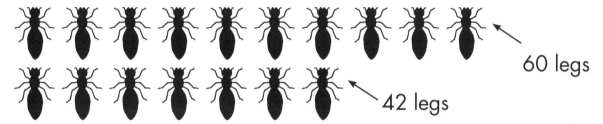

60 legs

42 legs

60 + 42 = 102
So, 17 ants have 102 legs altogether.

What is the total number of legs that 20 ants have?

What is the total number of legs that 13 ants have?

What is the total number of legs that 18 ants have?

What is the total number of legs that 15 ants have?

What is the total number of legs that 19 ants have?

Teacher's notes

Suggested objective: *Look for patterns in results and use these to find other results.*

Problem: *Can you use the ant times table?*
The children can use the 'ant times table' that they completed on sheet 38 to help them to solve the problems. You may wish to 'formalise' each question by writing it out as a number sentence after the children have found the answers. For example, you could show the children that the 17 ants question could be written out as 17 x 6 = 102. Ask the children to show working out on the back of this sheet.

Name _____ Date _____

Can you find multiples?

Instructions

1 Look at the hundred square below.

2 Mark all the multiples of 2 with a red dot.

3 Mark all the multiples of 5 with a blue dot.

1	2	3	4	5	6	7	8	9	10
11	12	13	14	15	16	17	18	19	20
21	22	23	24	25	26	27	28	29	30
31	32	33	34	35	36	37	38	39	40
41	42	43	44	45	46	47	48	49	50
51	52	53	54	55	56	57	58	59	60
61	62	63	64	65	66	67	68	69	70
71	72	73	74	75	76	77	78	79	80
81	82	83	84	85	86	87	88	89	90
91	92	93	94	95	96	97	98	99	100

Which numbers are multiples of 2 and 5?

[ ] [ ] [ ] [ ] [ ] [ ] [ ] [ ] [ ] [ ]

Can you see a pattern in your results?

Teacher's notes

Suggested objective: *Look for patterns in results and use these to find other results.*

Problem: *Can you find multiples?*
Encourage the children to work tidily and systematically so that it is easy for them to identify the squares that have both colours of dots – these are the squares that contain the common multiples of 2 and 5.

Can you find multiples?

Instructions

1 Look at the hundred square below.

2 Mark all the multiples of 3 with a red dot.

3 Mark all the multiples of 4 with a blue dot.

1	2	3	4	5	6	7	8	9	10
11	12	13	14	15	16	17	18	19	20
21	22	23	24	25	26	27	28	29	30
31	32	33	34	35	36	37	38	39	40
41	42	43	44	45	46	47	48	49	50
51	52	53	54	55	56	57	58	59	60
61	62	63	64	65	66	67	68	69	70
71	72	73	74	75	76	77	78	79	80
81	82	83	84	85	86	87	88	89	90
91	92	93	94	95	96	97	98	99	100

Which numbers are multiples of 3 and 4?

Can you see a pattern in your results?

Teacher's notes

Suggested objective: *Look for patterns in results and use these to find other results.*

Problem: *Can you find multiples?*

Encourage the children to work tidily and systematically so that it is easy for them to identify the squares that have both colours of dots – these are the squares that contain the common multiples of 3 and 4. Can they describe the pattern of results – what other multiples do these boxes contain?

Can you find multiples?

Instructions

1 Look at the hundred square below.

2 Mark all the multiples of 5 with a red dot.

3 Mark all the multiples of 6 with a blue dot.

1	2	3	4	5	6	7	8	9	10
11	12	13	14	15	16	17	18	19	20
21	22	23	24	25	26	27	28	29	30
31	32	33	34	35	36	37	38	39	40
41	42	43	44	45	46	47	48	49	50
51	52	53	54	55	56	57	58	59	60
61	62	63	64	65	66	67	68	69	70
71	72	73	74	75	76	77	78	79	80
81	82	83	84	85	86	87	88	89	90
91	92	93	94	95	96	97	98	99	100

Which numbers are multiples of 5 and 6?

☐ ☐ ☐

Can you see a pattern in your results?

Teacher's notes

Suggested objective: *Look for patterns in results and use these to find other results.*

Problem: *Can you find multiples?*
Encourage the children to work tidily and systematically so that it is easy for them to identify the squares that have both colours of dots – these are the squares that contain the common multiples of 5 and 6. Can they describe the pattern of results – what other multiples do these boxes contain?

Can you find multiples?

Instructions

1 Look at the hundred square below.

2 Mark all the multiples of 4 with a red dot.

3 Mark all the multiples of 6 with a blue dot.

1	2	3	4	5	6	7	8	9	10
11	12	13	14	15	16	17	18	19	20
21	22	23	24	25	26	27	28	29	30
31	32	33	34	35	36	37	38	39	40
41	42	43	44	45	46	47	48	49	50
51	52	53	54	55	56	57	58	59	60
61	62	63	64	65	66	67	68	69	70
71	72	73	74	75	76	77	78	79	80
81	82	83	84	85	86	87	88	89	90
91	92	93	94	95	96	97	98	99	100

Which numbers are multiples of 4 and 6?

☐ ☐ ☐ ☐ ☐ ☐ ☐ ☐

Can you see a pattern in your results?

Teacher's notes

Suggested objective: *Look for patterns in results and use these to find other results.*

Problem: *Can you find multiples?*

Encourage the children to work tidily and systematically so that it is easy for them to identify the squares that have both colours of dots – these are the squares that contain the common multiples of 4 and 6. Can they describe the pattern of results – what other multiples do these boxes contain?

Can you find pairs of multiples of 5 that make 100?

Look at the hundred square below.

1	2	3	4	5	6	7	8	9	10
11	12	13	14	15	16	17	18	19	20
21	22	23	24	25	26	27	28	29	30
31	32	33	34	35	36	37	38	39	40
41	42	43	44	45	46	47	48	49	50
51	52	53	54	55	56	57	58	59	60
61	62	63	64	65	66	67	68	69	70
71	72	73	74	75	76	77	78	79	80
81	82	83	84	85	86	87	88	89	90
91	92	93	94	95	96	97	98	99	100

If you colour five of the squares, how many are not coloured?

This shows that 5 + ☐ = 100

Can you find the other pairs of multiples of 5 that make 100?

Write your answers on the back of this sheet.

Teacher's notes

Suggested objective: *Look for patterns in results and use these to find other results.*

Problem: *Can you find pairs of multiples of 5 that make 100?*

Encourage the children to work tidily and systematically so that it is easy for them to find all the combinations of multiples of 5.

You could use the patterns as a focus for a class mental arithmetic discussion, using questions such as 100 – 35, 100 – 25, 100 – 45, 100 – 85, etc. Once the children are confident with answering these, ask questions such as 100 – 3, 100 – 23, 100 – 73, etc. Look out for those who answer a question such as 100 – 64 with the incorrect answer 46 as they have followed some patterns incorrectly: they know that 100 – 60 = 40 and that 10 – 6 = 4 but they have combined their results incorrectly. A number line will help to overcome this difficulty.

Can you find how much string is left?

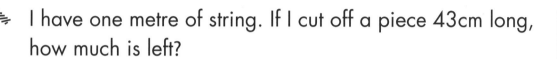

I have one metre of string. If I cut off a piece 43cm long, how much is left?

I have one metre of string. If I cut off a piece 69cm long, how much is left?

I have one metre of string. If I cut off a piece 76cm long, how much is left?

I have one metre of string. If I cut off a piece 99cm long, how much is left?

I have one metre of string. If I cut off a piece 16cm long, how much is left?

I have one metre of string. If I cut off a piece 28cm long, how much is left?

Teacher's notes

Suggested objective: *Look for patterns in results and use these to find other results.*

Problem: *Can you find how much string is left of a metre length of string when a piece is cut off?*
The children need to interpret the wording of each question then use their knowledge of the pattern of results found when combining pairs of numbers to make 100.

Discussion sheet: Can you find pairs of multiples of 5 that make 60?

You can see that the clock face is shaded as far as 35 minutes. How many minutes are there left to shade?

This shows that 35 + ⬚ = 60

Teacher's notes

Suggested objective: *Look for patterns in results and use these to find other results.*

Problem: *Can you find pairs of multiples of 5 that make 60?*

Discuss strategies with the children and ensure that they understand the information shown by the shaded clock face. When you feel they are ready, give them a copy of sheet 47, which has an unshaded clock face. You could use the patterns as a focus for a class mental arithmetic discussion, using questions such as 60 – 35, 60 – 25, 60 – 45, 60 – 15, etc.

Andrew Brodie: Solving Maths Problems 7–9 © A&C Black 2010

Can you find pairs of multiples of 5 that make 60?

Look at the clock face.

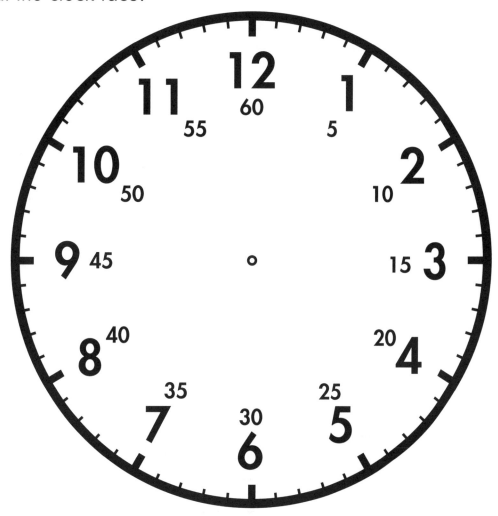

Can you find the pairs of multiples of 5 that make 60?
Write your answers on the back of this sheet.

Teacher's notes

Suggested objective: *Look for patterns in results and use these to find other results.*

Problem: *Can you find pairs of multiples of 5 that make 60?*
This activity should follow the discussion work on sheet 46. Encourage the children to work tidily and systematically so that it is easy for them to find all the combinations of multiples of 5.

How much time is left?

A one-hour television programme started at 3 o'clock.
For how many minutes has
the programme been on?

How many more minutes will
the programme be on for?

A one-hour television programme started at 7 o'clock.
For how many minutes has
the programme been on?

How many more minutes will
the programme be on for?

A one-hour television programme started at 11 o'clock.
For how many minutes has
the programme been on?

How many more minutes will
the programme be on for?

Teacher's notes

Suggested objective: *Look for patterns in results and use these to find other results.*

Problem: *Can you find how much time is left?*
Children look at each clock and answer the questions above. They need to interpret the wording of each question then use their knowledge of the pattern of results found when combining pairs of numbers to make 60.

Name _____ Date _____

What time is it?

What time does the clock show?

What time will it be 15 minutes after this time?

What time does the clock show?

What time was it 15 minutes before this time?

What time does the clock show?

What time will it be 5 minutes after this time?

Teacher's notes

Suggested objective: *Look for patterns in results and use these to find other results.*

Problem: *What time is it?*
The children need to interpret the wording of each question then use the appropriate vocabulary or number representation to show the correct time and the related time as asked by the question.

Name _____ Date _____

What time is it?

What time does the clock show?

[   ]

What time will it be 15 minutes after this time?

[   ]

What time does the clock show?

[   ]

What time was it 15 minutes before this time?

[   ]

What time does the clock show?

[   ]

What time will it be 5 minutes after this time?

[   ]

Teacher's notes

Suggested objective: *Look for patterns in results and use these to find other results.*

Problem: *What time is it?*

The children need to interpret the wording of each question then use the appropriate vocabulary or number representation to show the correct time and the related time as asked by the question.

What time is it?

What time does the clock show?

[   ]

What time will it be 25 minutes after this time?

[   ]

What time does the clock show?

[   ]

What time was it 25 minutes before this time?

[   ]

What time does the clock show?

[   ]

What time will it be 25 minutes after this time?

[   ]

Teacher's notes

Suggested objective: *Look for patterns in results and use these to find other results.*

Problem: *What time is it?*
The children need to interpret the wording of each question then use the appropriate vocabulary or number representation to show the correct time and the related time as asked by the question.

Name _____ Date _____

What time is it?

What time does the clock show?

[ ]

What time will it be 30 minutes after this time?

[ ]

What time does the clock show?

[ ]

What time was it 30 minutes before this time?

[ ]

What time does the clock show?

[ ]

What time will it be 30 minutes after this time?

[ ]

Teacher's notes

Suggested objective: *Look for patterns in results and use these to find other results.*

Problem: *What time is it?*

The children need to interpret the wording of each question then use the appropriate vocabulary or number representation to show the correct time and the related time as asked by the question.

Discussion sheet: What shapes can you find?

What other shapes can you find by drawing a straight line from one corner of a shape to another corner?

Look at the square:

We can draw a line from one corner of the square to another to make two triangles.

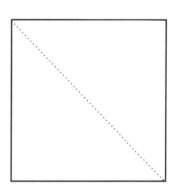

What shapes can you make when you draw a straight line from one corner of a pentagon to another corner?

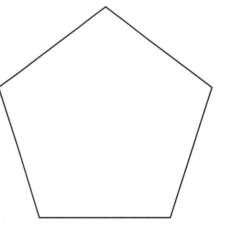

Teacher's notes

Suggested objective: *Investigate shapes and use correct vocabulary.*

Problem: *What shapes can you find?*

This discussion sheet provides an introduction to the activities on sheets 54 and 55 as well as giving opportunities for revising appropriate vocabulary for shape work.

What shapes can you find?

What other shapes can you find by drawing a straight line from one corner of a **hexagon** to another corner?

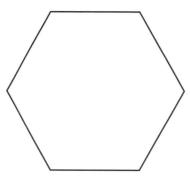

Now draw a line from the same corner to a different corner. What different shapes can you find now?

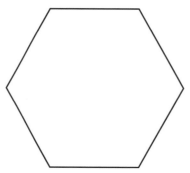

What shapes can you find if you draw more than one line? Investigate with these hexagons:

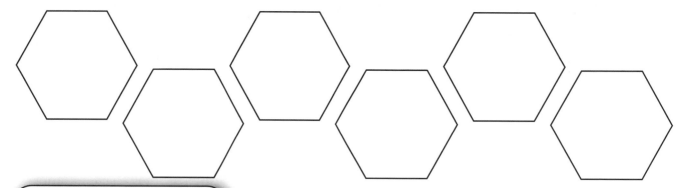

Teacher's notes

Suggested objective: *Investigate shapes and use correct vocabulary.*

Problem: *What shapes can you find?*
Encourage the children to investigate by drawing lines. As with all good investigations there are no right or wrong results – every result should be considered as valid and should encourage useful discussion.

What shapes can you find?

What other shapes can you find by drawing a straight line from one corner of an **octagon** to another corner?

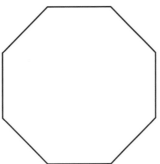

What different shapes do you find when you draw a line from the same corner as above but to a different corner?

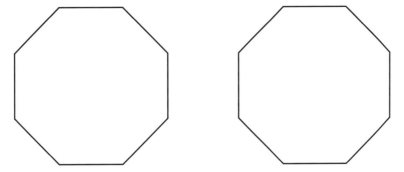

What shapes can you find if you draw more than one line? Investigate with these octagons:

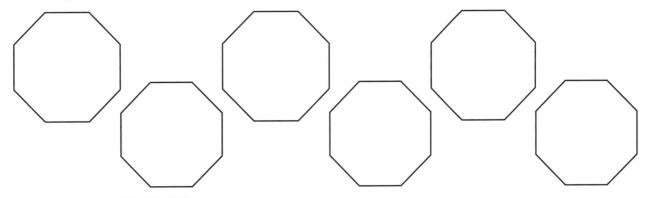

Discussion sheet: What are these shapes?

Teacher's notes

Suggested objective: *Investigate shapes and use correct vocabulary.*

Problem: *What are these shapes?*

Discuss the shapes and their attributes. Ask questions such as: How many sides? How many corners? Does the shape have any right angles? What is special about the shape?

Ask the children to cut out the shapes carefully so that they can be used with sheet 67.

Andrew Brodie: Solving Maths Problems 7-9 © A&C Black 2010

Can you sort the shapes?

Use the Carroll diagram to sort the shapes that you cut out on Sheet 56. Can you find a place for all of the shapes?

Has at least one right angle	Does not have any right angles
Has 4 sides	**Does not have 4 sides**

Teacher's notes

Suggested objective: *Investigate shapes and use correct vocabulary.*

Problem: *Can you sort the shapes?*

Discuss the shapes from sheet 56 considering their attributes. Ask questions such as: How many sides? How many corners? Does the shape have any right angles? What is special about the shape? Support the children in sorting the shapes into the appropriate sections of the Carroll diagram.

Can you interpret the bar chart?

Eliza counted the number of each type of book on one shelf of the class library. She drew a bar chart to show what she found.

Books on the shelf

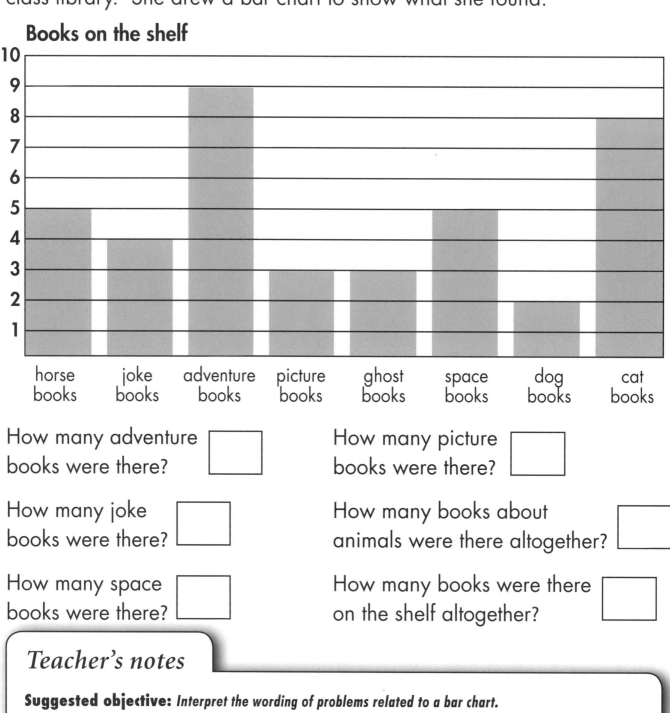

How many adventure books were there? ☐

How many picture books were there? ☐

How many joke books were there? ☐

How many books about animals were there altogether? ☐

How many space books were there? ☐

How many books were there on the shelf altogether? ☐

Teacher's notes

Suggested objective: *Interpret the wording of problems related to a bar chart.*

Problem: *Can you interpret the bar chart?*
The children answer the questions above using the information in the bar chart.

Andrew Brodie: Solving Maths Problems 7–9 © A&C Black 2010

Can you interpret the bar chart?

Callum asked people about the pets they have.
He drew a bar chart to show what he found.

Pets at home

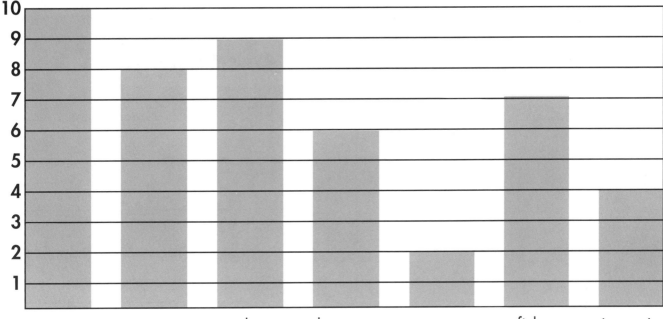

How many people have guinea-pigs? [ ]

How many people have fish? [ ]

How many people don't have a pet at home? [ ]

How many more people own hamsters than rats? [ ]

Which is the most popular pet? [ ]

Which is the least popular pet? [ ]

Name _____ Date _____

How far can you double?

Double 2 = 4 ➝ **Double 4 = 8** ➝

Now find double 8. Write your answer in the box below, then continue doubling. Then do the same with double 3.

Doubling from 2

Double 2 = 4

Double 4 = 8

_____

_____

_____

_____

_____

_____

Doubling from 3

Double 3 = _____

_____

_____

_____

_____

_____

_____

Teacher's notes

Suggested objective: *Use patterns to find other outcomes.*

Problem: *How far can you double?*
This sheet encourages children to stretch their own number skills and to observe the effect of doubling.
Are they surprised how quickly the numbers grow in size?

How far can you double?

Double 5 = 10 ⟶ **Double 10 = 20** ⟶

Now find double 20. Write your answer in the box below, then continue doubling. Then do the same with double 7.

Doubling from 5	**Doubling from 7**
Double 5 = 10	Double 7 = _____
Double 10 = 20	

Teacher's notes

Suggested objective: *Use patterns to find other outcomes.*

Problem: *How far can you double?*
This sheet encourages children to stretch their own number skills and to observe the effect of doubling. Are they surprised how quickly the numbers grow in size?

Andrew Brodie: Solving Maths Problems 7–9 © A&C Black 2010

Can you make the heptagon times table?

1 heptagon ⬡ ←7 corners

2 heptagons ⬡⬡ ←14 corners

3 heptagons ⬡⬡⬡ ☐ corners

4 heptagons ⬡⬡⬡⬡ ☐ corners

5 heptagons ⬡⬡⬡⬡⬡ ☐ corners

6 heptagons ⬡⬡⬡⬡⬡⬡ ☐ corners

7 heptagons ⬡⬡⬡⬡⬡⬡⬡ ☐ corners

8 heptagons ⬡⬡⬡⬡⬡⬡⬡⬡ ☐ corners

9 heptagons ⬡⬡⬡⬡⬡⬡⬡⬡⬡ ☐ corners

10 heptagons ⬡⬡⬡⬡⬡⬡⬡⬡⬡⬡ ☐
corners

Teacher's notes

Suggested objective: *Look for patterns in results and use these to find other results.*

Problem: *Can you make the heptagon times table?*

Ensure that the children know the term 'heptagon' for a seven-sided shape – you may wish to show them a 20p or a 50p coin, both of which are based on heptagons though are not true heptagons as their sides are not straight.

This is, of course, the seven times table derived from considering the total number of corners for each set of heptagons. The advantage of creating the table in this way is that the products can be related to real 'objects', i.e. the corners of the heptagons. Many children find this an easier concept, particularly when they need to apply the results to further problems – these problems are provided on sheet 63.

Using the heptagon times table

Example:

What is the total number of corners that 16 heptagons have?

We know that 10 heptagons have 70 corners altogether and that 6 heptagons have 42 corners altogether:

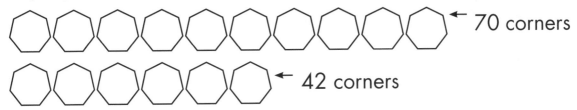

← 70 corners

← 42 corners

70 + 42 = 112   So, 16 heptagons have 112 corners altogether.

What is the total number of corners that 20 heptagons have? ☐

What is the total number of corners that 13 heptagons have? ☐

What is the total number of corners that 17 heptagons have? ☐

What is the total number of corners that 11 heptagons have? ☐

What is the total number of corners that 19 heptagons have? ☐

What is the total number of corners that 30 heptagons have? ☐

Teacher's notes

Suggested objective: *Look for patterns in results and use these to find other results.*

Problem: *Can you use the heptagon times table?*
The children can use the 'heptagon times table' that they completed on sheet 62 to help them to solve the problems. You may wish to 'formalise' each question by writing it out as a number sentence after the children have found the answers. For example, you could show the children that the 16 heptagons question could be written out as 16 x 7 = 112.
Extension Problem: Ask the children if they can find the number of corners of any number of heptagons. Can they suggest how they would approach this?

Can you make the spider times table?

1 spider ← 8 legs

2 spiders ← 16 legs

3 spiders [ ] legs

4 spiders [ ] legs

5 spiders [ ] legs

6 spiders [ ] legs

7 spiders [ ] legs

8 spiders [ ] legs

9 spiders [ ] legs

10 spiders [ ] legs

Teacher's notes

Suggested objective: *Look for patterns in results and use these to find other results.*

Problem: *Can you make the spider times table?*
This is, of course, the eight times table derived from considering the total number of legs for each set of spiders. The advantage of creating the table in this way is that the products can be related to real 'objects', ie the legs of the spiders. Many children find this an easier concept, particularly when they need to apply the results to further problems – these problems are provided on sheet 65.

Andrew Brodie: Solving Maths Problems 7–9 © A&C Black 2010

Name _____ Date _____

Using the spider times table Sheet 65

Example:
What is the total number of legs that 15 spiders have?

We know that 10 spiders have 80 legs altogether and that 5 spiders have 40 legs altogether:

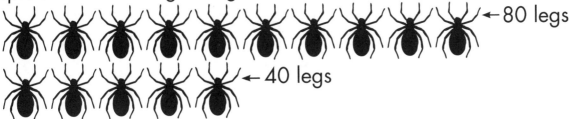
←80 legs
←40 legs

80 + 40 = 120   So, 15 spiders have 120 legs altogether.

What is the total number of legs that 18 spiders have? ☐

What is the total number of legs that 12 spiders have? ☐

What is the total number of legs that 17 spiders have? ☐

What is the total number of legs that 14 spiders have? ☐

What is the total number of legs that 20 spiders have? ☐

What is the total number of legs that 40 spiders have? ☐

Teacher's notes

Suggested objective: *Look for patterns in results and use these to find other results.*

Problem: *Can you use the spider times table?*
The children can use the 'spider times table' that they completed on sheet 64 to help them to solve the problems. You may wish to 'formalise' each question by writing it out as a number sentence after the children have found the answers. For example, you could show the children that the 15 spiders question could be written out as 15 x 8 = 120.
Extension Problem: Ask the children if they can find the number of legs of any number of spiders. Can they suggest how they would approach this?

75

Can you make the nonagon times table?

1 nonagon ⬡ ← 9 corners

2 nonagons ⬡⬡ ← 18 corners

3 nonagons ⬡⬡⬡ ▭ corners

4 nonagons ⬡⬡⬡⬡ ▭ corners

5 nonagons ⬡⬡⬡⬡⬡ ▭ corners

6 nonagons ⬡⬡⬡⬡⬡⬡ ▭ corners

7 nonagons ⬡⬡⬡⬡⬡⬡⬡ ▭ corners

8 nonagons ⬡⬡⬡⬡⬡⬡⬡⬡ ▭ corners

9 nonagons ⬡⬡⬡⬡⬡⬡⬡⬡⬡ ▭ corners

10 nonagons ⬡⬡⬡⬡⬡⬡⬡⬡⬡⬡ ▭ corners

Teacher's notes

Suggested objective: *Look for patterns in results and use these to find other results.*

Problem: *Can you make the nonagon times table?*

Ensure that the children know the term 'nonagon' for a nine-sided shape. This is, of course, the nine times table derived from considering the total number of corners for each set of nonagons. The advantage of creating the table in this way is that the products can be related to real 'objects', i.e. the corners of the nonagons. Many children find this an easier concept, particularly when they need to apply the results to further problems – these problems are provided on sheet 67.

Using the nonagon times table

Example:

What is the total number of corners that 18 nonagons have?

We know that 10 nonagons have 90 corners altogether and that 8 nonagons have 72 corners altogether:

← 90 corners

← 72 corners

90 + 72 = 162   So, 18 nonagons have 162 corners altogether.

What is the total number of corners that 13 nonagons have? ☐

What is the total number of corners that 20 nonagons have? ☐

What is the total number of corners that 30 nonagons have? ☐

What is the total number of corners that 32 nonagons have? ☐

What is the total number of corners that 51 nonagons have? ☐

What is the total number of corners that 64 nonagons have? ☐

Teacher's notes

Suggested objective: *Look for patterns in results and use these to find other results.*

Problem: *Can you use the nonagon times table?*
The children can use the 'nonagon times table' that they completed on sheet 66 to help them to solve the problems. You may wish to 'formalise' each question by writing it out as a number sentence after the children have found the answers. For example, you could show the children that the 18 nonagons question could be written out as 18 x 9 = 162.
Extension Problem: Ask the children if they feel they can find the number of corners of any number of nonagons. Can they suggest how they would approach this?

Andrew Brodie: Solving Maths Problems 7-9 © A&C Black 2010

Discussion sheet: How many connections can you make?

3 x 2 = 6

We can use this fact to find other calculation sentences.

Here are some examples:

6 ÷ 2 = 3

2 x 3 = 6

30 x 2 = 60

2 x 30 = 60

Can you find any others?

Teacher's notes

Suggested objective: *Use patterns to find other outcomes.*

Problem: *How many connections can you make between three numbers?*
Are the children looking for patterns in results? Do they use these to find other results? Do they understand place value in numbers to 1000? Can they use mental recall of addition and subtraction facts to 20 in solving problems involving larger numbers?

How many connections can you make?

$$5 \times 4 = 20$$

We can use this fact to find other calculation sentences.

Here are some examples:

$$20 \div 4 = 5$$

$$5 \times 40 = 200$$

$$50 \times 40 = 2000$$

Find some connected calculations for each of those given below.

$6 \times 3 = 18$	$4 \times 9 = 36$	$5 \times 2 = 10$
_____	_____	_____
_____	_____	_____
_____	_____	_____
_____	_____	_____
_____	_____	_____

Teacher's notes

Suggested objective: *Use patterns to find other outcomes.*

Problem: *How many connections can you make between three numbers?*
Are the children looking for patterns in results? Do they use these to find other results? Do they understand place value in numbers to 1000 and beyond? Can they use mental recall of multiplication facts in solving problems involving divisions and larger numbers?

Name _____ Date _____

How many connections can you make?

$$50 \div 5 = 10$$

We can use this fact to find other calculation sentences.

Here are some examples:

$$50 \div 10 = 5$$
$$5 \times 10 = 50$$
$$10 \times 50 = 500$$

Find some connected calculations for each of those given below.

$42 \div 6 = 7$	$72 \div 9 = 8$	$100 \div 10 = 10$
_____	_____	_____
_____	_____	_____
_____	_____	_____
_____	_____	_____
_____	_____	_____

Teacher's notes

Suggested objective: *Use patterns to find other outcomes.*

Problem: *How many connections can you make between three numbers?*
Are the children looking for patterns in results? Do they use these to find other results? Do they understand place value in numbers to 1000 and beyond? Can they use mental recall of multiplication facts in solving problems involving divisions and larger numbers?

Can you solve balance problems?

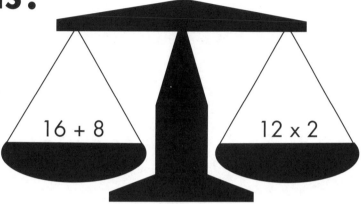

16 + 8   12 x 2

The scales are balanced because both calculations have the same answer.

Find the missing number to write in each box. Remember, both sides of the equals sign (=) must balance.

10 + 14 = 8 x [   ]   3 x 9 = 13 + [   ]

4 x 8 = 10 + [   ]   13 + 17 = [   ] x 5

34 + 6 = [   ] x 8   42 + 18 = [   ] x 6

6 x [   ] = 16 + 38   7 x [   ] = 40 + 16

8 x [   ] = 2 x 36   [   ] + 30 = 9 x 7

[   ] + 12 = 7 x 6   [   ] + 15 = 6 x 8

Teacher's notes

Suggested objective: *Solve 'balancing' problems.*

Problem: *Can you make both sides of the equals sign balance?*
Are the children beginning to understand the role of the equals sign? Many children assume that the equals sign leads to an 'answer' but they will find much of their later maths work much easier if they understand that the equals sign indicates a balance of values. Help them to see that each of these 'balancing problems' can be solved by finding the value of one side, then making the other side worth the same.

Name _____ **Date** _____

Can you solve balance problems?

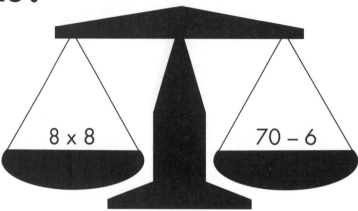

8 x 8   70 – 6

The scales are balanced because both calculations have the same answer.

Find the missing number to write in each box. Remember, both sides of the equals sign (=) must balance.

7 x 9 = 70 – ☐

8 x 9 = 100 – ☐

5 x 7 = ☐ – 15

40 – ☐ = 6 x 4

42 – ☐ = 6 x 6

☐ – 7 = 4 x 9

4 x 8 = 40 – ☐

3 x 9 = ☐ – 13

7 x 8 = ☐ – 20

64 – ☐ = 5 x 9

☐ – 19 = 9 x 9

☐ – 12 = 8 x 5

Teacher's notes

Suggested objective: *Solve 'balancing' problems.*

Problem: *Can you make both sides of the equals sign balance?*

Help the children to see that each of these 'balancing problems' can be solved by finding the value of one side, then making the other side worth the same.

Andrew Brodie: Solving Maths Problems 7-9 © A&C Black 2010

Can you solve balance problems?

Sheet 73

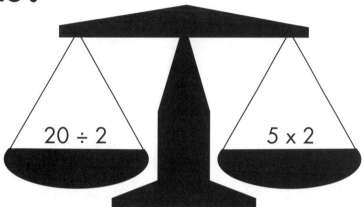

The scales are balanced because both calculations have the same answer.

Find the missing number to write in each box. Remember, both sides of the equals sign (=) must balance.

$40 \div 2 = 4 \times \boxed{}$

$42 \div 7 = 15 - \boxed{}$

$72 \div 9 = \boxed{} - 5$

$48 \div \boxed{} = 12 - 4$

$100 \div \boxed{} = 40 - 15$

$\boxed{} \div 4 = 4 \times 5$

$32 \div 8 = 12 - \boxed{}$

$56 \div 8 = \boxed{} - 9$

$54 \div 6 = \boxed{} - 11$

$81 \div \boxed{} = 30 - 21$

$\boxed{} \div 2 = 9 \times 2$

$\boxed{} \div 2 = 7 \times 3$

Teacher's notes

Suggested objective: *Solve 'balancing' problems.*

Problem: *Can you make both sides of the equals sign balance?*
Help the children to see that each of these 'balancing problems' can be solved by finding the value of one side, then making the other side worth the same.

Can you solve balance problems?

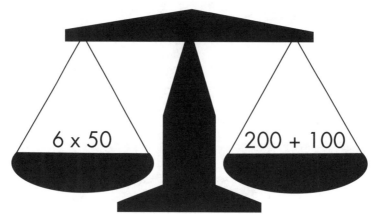

The scales are balanced because both calculations have the same answer.

Find the missing number to write in each box. Remember, both sides of the equals sign (=) must balance.

4 x 50 = 10 x ☐

4 x 25 = 20 + ☐

9 x 30 = ☐ + 60

9 x ☐ = 100 + 80

8 x ☐ = 300 – 60

☐ x 70 = 500 – 80

8 x 20 = 200 – ☐

6 x 40 = ☐ + 20

8 x 50 = ☐ – 100

10 x ☐ = 1000 – 400

☐ x 20 = 120 – 0

☐ x 30 = 300 – 90

Teacher's notes

Suggested objective: *Solve 'balancing' problems.*

Problem: *Can you make both sides of the equals sign balance?*
Help the children to see that each of these 'balancing problems' can be solved by finding the value of one side, then making the other side worth the same.

Discussion sheet: What number am I thinking of?

I think of a number. I double it. I add 3. The answer is 25. What number did I first think of?

Teacher's notes

Suggested objective: *Use inverses to find missing numbers in word problems.*

Problem: *What number am I thinking of?*

This sheet is designed to form an introduction to a set of activities in which the pupils have to use inverse calculations to find missing numbers.

Are the children looking for patterns in results? Do they use these to find other results? Can the children derive associated division facts from known multiplication facts? Can the children use mental recall of addition and subtraction facts to 20 in solving problems involving larger numbers? Do they understand halving as a way of 'undoing' doubling and vice versa?

What number am I thinking of?

I think of a number. I double it. I add 7. The answer is 19.

What number did I first think of?

I think of a number. I double it. I add 12. The answer is 30.

What number did I first think of?

I think of a number. I double it. I add 8. The answer is 24.

What number did I first think of?

I think of a number. I double it. I add 10. The answer is 40.

What number did I first think of?

Teacher's notes

Suggested objective: *Use inverses to find missing numbers in word problems.*

Problem: *What number am I thinking of?*

Are the children looking for patterns in results? Do they use these to find other results? Can the children derive associated division facts from known multiplication facts? Can the children use mental recall of addition and subtraction facts to 20 in solving problems involving larger numbers? Do they understand halving as a way of 'undoing' doubling and vice versa? Many children will find this concept quite difficult but those who are confident could make up some of their own problems like the ones on the sheet. They could share these with other confident children.

Andrew Brodie: Solving Maths Problems 7-9 © A&C Black 2010

What number am I thinking of?

I think of a number.
I halve it. I subtract 4.
The answer is 6.

What number did
I first think of?

I think of a number.
I halve it. I subtract 6.
The answer is 5.

What number did
I first think of?

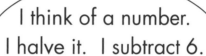

I think of a number.
I halve it. I subtract 8.
The answer is 4.

What number did
I first think of?

I think of a number.
I halve it. I subtract 10.
The answer is 2.

What number did
I first think of?

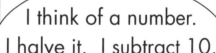

Teacher's notes

Suggested objective: *Use inverses to find missing numbers in word problems.*

Problem: *What number am I thinking of?*
Are the children looking for patterns in results? Do they use these to find other results? Can the children derive associated division facts from known multiplication facts? Can the children use mental recall of addition and subtraction facts to 20 in solving problems involving larger numbers? Do they understand halving as a way of 'undoing' doubling and vice versa? Many children will find this concept quite difficult but those who are confident could make up some of their own problems like the ones on the sheet. They could share these with other confident children.

What number am I thinking of?

I think of a number.
I add 7. I multiply by 3.
The answer is 27.

What number did
I first think of?

I think of a number.
I add 4. I multiply by 5.
The answer is 50.

What number did
I first think of?

I think of a number.
I add 2. I multiply by 4.
The answer is 36.

What number did
I first think of?

I think of a number.
I add 8. I multiply by 2.
The answer is 24.

What number did
I first think of?

Teacher's notes

Suggested objective: *Use inverses to find missing numbers in word problems.*

Problem: *What number am I thinking of?*

Are the children looking for patterns in results? Do they use these to find other results? Can the children derive associated division facts from known multiplication facts? Can the children use mental recall of addition and subtraction facts to 20 in solving problems involving larger numbers? Do they understand halving as a way of 'undoing' doubling and vice versa? Many children will find this concept quite difficult but those who are confident could make up some of their own problems like the ones on the sheet. They could share these with other confident children.

Name _____ Date _____

What number am I thinking of?

I think of a number. I multiply by 3. I divide by 2. The answer is 9.

What number did I first think of?

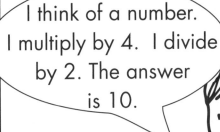

I think of a number. I multiply by 4. I divide by 2. The answer is 10.

What number did I first think of?

I think of a number. I multiply by 5. I divide by 2. The answer is 20.

What number did I first think of?

I think of a number. I multiply by 2. I divide by 4. The answer is 6.

What number did I first think of?

Teacher's notes

Suggested objective: *Use inverses to find missing numbers in word problems.*

Problem: *What number am I thinking of?*
Are the children looking for patterns in results? Do they use these to find other results? Can the children derive associated division facts from known multiplication facts? Do they understand halving as a way of 'undoing' doubling and vice versa? Many children will find this concept quite difficult but those who are confident could make up some of their own problems like the ones on the sheet. They could share these with other confident children.

Which is the best value?

Tom bought 3 apples for 60p.

Will bought 5 apples for 90p.

Who had the best value for money?

Show how you worked this out.

Teacher's notes

Suggested objective: *Develop an organised approach to solving a problem.*

Problem: *Which is the best value?*

The idea of finding best value may be familiar to the pupils from everyday shopping activities but ask them *how* they can carry out the process. Some pupils may be able to state that finding the cost of one item from each set will allow a comparison to be made. You could provide the children with coins to investigate the solutions.

Which is the best value?

Amy bought 4 bars of chocolate for £1.80.

Ann bought 7 bars of chocolate for £3.50.

Who had the best value for money?

Show how you worked this out.

Andrew Brodie: Solving Maths Problems 7-9 © A&C Black 2010

Name _____ Date _____

What can we afford?

lemonade 35p

cola 55p

flapjack 60p

shortbread 70p

I have £5.

I have 4 friends. We have all decided that we will have the same drink and the same biscuit. What can we afford?

How many combinations can we make?

lemonade 35p   shortbread 70p

cola 55p

flapjack 60p

chocolate
cake 90p

I have 4 friends. We are each going to have a drink and a cake.
We have decided that no two people are going to have the same
combination of food and drink. Can you find all the different
combinations?

Which is the most expensive combination?

Which is the least expensive combination?

Teacher's notes

Suggested objective: *Developing an organised approach to solving a problem.*

Problem: *How many combinations can we make?*
As with finding best value, the concept here will be familiar to the pupils from everyday shopping activities
but again, ask them *how* they can carry out the process.

Name _____ Date _____

How much change will we get?

orange juice 75p

apple juice 60p

crispy cake 80p

carrot cake 90p

muffin 85p

I have 3 friends. We have a £10 note. We are each going to have a drink and a cake.

Which is the most expensive combination of drink and cake in this café?

Which is the least expensive combination of drink and cake in this café?

If we all have the most expensive combination, what change would we get from £10?

If we all have the least expensive combination, what change would we get from £10?

Teacher's notes

Suggested objective: *Developing an organised approach to solving a problem.*

Problem: *How much change will we get?*
This is a very challenging sheet as the pupils will need to take several steps to find the answers to the final two questions. They will have to decide which calculations to use and they will have to be accurate when calculating.

Andrew Brodie: Solving Maths Problems 7–9 © A&C Black 2010

Discussion sheet: What uniform do boys need?

shorts £6.50

socks, pack of five pairs £6

trousers £8

shirts, pack of three £9

sweatshirt £4

jumper £9

polo shirts, pack of three £7.50

Teacher's notes

This activity sheet to be used in conjunction with Sheets 87 and 88.
Suggested objective: *Solve one-step and two-step problems involving money.*

Problem: *What uniform do boys need?*
Look at the clothing items with the children. Which items do boys need for school? Which items would they choose, where there is a choice? What is the cost of each shirt in a multi-pack? What is the cost of each pair of socks in a multi-pack?

Andrew Brodie: Solving Maths Problems 7–9 © A&C Black 2010

Name _____ Date _____

Discussion sheet: What uniform do girls need?

 tights, three pairs £4.50

 jumper £9

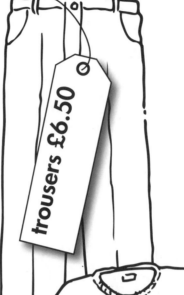 trousers £6.50

 summer dress £6

 long-sleeved blouse, pack of two £5

sweatshirt £4

 skirt £8

 short-sleeved blouse, pack of three £7.50

socks, pack of five pairs £6

Teacher's notes

This activity sheet to be used in conjunction with Sheets 87 and 88.
Suggested objective: *Solve one-step and two-step problems involving money.*

Problem: *What uniform do girls need?*
Look at the clothing items with the children. Which items do girls need for school? Which items would they choose, where there is a choice? What is the cost of each item in a multi-pack?

What uniform do I need?

Look at the choices of uniform items on Sheets 85 and 86. You have
£40 to spend on your school uniform. Which items would you buy?
What would the total cost be? How much money would you have left?

Total cost =		
Money left out of £40 =		

Teacher's notes

This activity sheet to be used in conjunction with Sheets 85 and 86.
Suggested objective: *Solve one-step and two-step problems involving money.*

Problem: *What uniform do I need?*
Discuss the boys' and girls' clothing items with the children that are on sheets 85 and 86. Which items do they
need for school? Which items would they choose, where there is a choice?
How do the children set out their work? How do they make use of the table? Do they work systematically?

Andrew Brodie: Solving Maths Problems 7-9 © A&C Black 2010

How do the prices compare?

Here are the price lists from boys' and girls' uniforms.

BOYS' UNIFORM LIST

trousers	£8
shorts	£6.50
shirts (pack of three)	£9
jumper	£9
sweatshirt	£4
polo-shirt (pack of three)	£7.50
socks (pack of five pairs)	£6

GIRLS' UNIFORM LIST

trousers £6.50

skirt £8

summer dress £6

jumper £9

sweatshirt £4

short-sleeved blouse (pack of three) £7.50

long-sleeved blouse (pack of two) £5

socks (pack of five pairs) £6

tights (three pairs) £4.50

How much cheaper are the girls' trousers than the boys' trousers? ☐

How much more expensive is a skirt than a pair of shorts? ☐

How much cheaper is a summer dress than a skirt? ☐

How much cheaper are three polo-shirts than three shirts? ☐

How much more expensive is one pair of tights than one pair of socks? ☐

Teacher's notes

Suggested objective: *Solve one-step and two-step problems involving money.*

Problem: *How do the prices compare?*

Discuss the girls' and boys' clothing items with the children. Which items are the same price as each other? Why do they think the blouses are cheaper than the shirts? Note that the final question involves several stages.

Andrew Brodie: Solving Maths Problems 7-9 © A&C Black 2010

Discussion sheet: What can I buy at the sports shop?

Basketball £4.99

Badminton shuttlecocks, three pack £3.99

Basketball ring with net £19.99

Netball post with net £55

Badminton racket £9.99

Goalkeeper's gloves £6.99

Netball £3

Junior tennis racket £14.99

Football goal £40

Football £4

Tennis balls, four pack £4.99

Teacher's notes

This activity sheet to be used in conjunction with Sheets 90-94.
Suggested objective: *Solve one-step and two-step problems involving money.*

Problem: *What can I buy at the sports shop?*
Look at the sports items with the children. Which items would they choose? What is the cost of each item in a multi-pack? (Note that this question will require some approximation for the multipack of tennis balls.) Which items cost more than £10?

Andrew Brodie: Solving Maths Problems 7-9 © A&C Black 2010

Name _____ **Date** _____

What can I buy at the sports shop?

Imagine you have won a £50 prize to spend in the sports shop!

Answer all of these questions:

Which item costs more than your prize money?

_____

Which items would you buy?

_____

_____

_____

_____

What would they cost altogether?

_____

Would you have to put in any extra money?

_____

Would you have some money left to spend another day? How much?

_____

working out space

Teacher's notes

This activity sheet to be used in conjunction with Sheet 89.
Suggested objective: *Solve one-step and two-step problems involving money.*

Problem: *What can I buy at the sports shop?*
Look at the sports items on sheet 89 with the children. Which items would they choose to buy with £50?
How can they find the total cost of their shopping spree?

Andrew Brodie: Solving Maths Problems 7–9 © A&C Black 2010

What can the PE teacher buy?

The new PE teacher wants to buy two football goals and ten footballs. How much will the football equipment cost altogether?

answer:

Football goal £40

Football £4

Netball £3

Netball post with net £55

The new PE teacher wants to buy two netball posts and ten netballs. How much will the netball equipment cost altogether?

answer:

How much will all the new sports equipment cost altogether?

answer:

Teacher's notes

Suggested objective: *Solve one-step and two-step problems involving money.*

Problem: *What can the PE teacher buy at the sports shop?*
Discuss the school's need for sports items with the children. How can they work out the total costs? Ask the children to use the back of this sheet to do their working out.

Andrew Brodie: Solving Maths Problems 7-9 © A&C Black 2010

How do the prices compare?

Here is the price list from the sports shop:

SPORTS SHOP PRICES:

Badminton shuttlecocks (three pack)	£3.99
Badminton racket	£9.99
Basketball ring with net	£19.99
Basketball	£4.99
Football	£4
Goalkeeper's gloves	£6.99
Football goal	£40
Junior tennis racket	£14.99
Tennis balls (four pack)	£4.99
Netball post with net	£55
Netball	£3

How much more is a football than a netball?

How much less than a junior tennis racket is a badminton racket?

How much more is a basketball than a netball?

How much more is a netball post than a football goal?

How much less than a football goal is a basketball ring with net?

Teacher's notes

Suggested objective: *Solve one-step and two-step problems involving money.*

Problem: *How do the prices compare?*

Look at the sports items on sheet 89 with the children. Why do they think some items are more expensive than others? Can they think of a quick way of dealing with prices that end with 99p? Ask the children to use the back of this sheet to do their working out.

Andrew Brodie: Solving Maths Problems 7–9 © A&C Black 2010

What do two cost?

Here is the price list from the sports shop:

SPORTS SHOP PRICES:

Badminton shuttlecocks (three pack)	£3.99
Badminton racket	£9.99
Basketball ring with net	£19.99
Basketball	£4.99
Football	£4
Goalkeeper's gloves	£6.99
Football goal	£40
Junior tennis racket	£14.99
Tennis balls (four pack)	£4.99
Netball post with net	£55
Netball	£3

What do 2 netballs cost altogether?

What do 2 footballs cost altogether?

What do 2 basketballs cost altogether?

What do 2 pairs of goalkeeper's gloves cost altogether?

What do 2 junior tennis rackets cost altogether?

Teacher's notes

Suggested objective: *Solve one-step and two-step problems involving money.*

Problem: *What do two cost?*
Look at the sports items on sheet 89 with the children. Can they think of a quick way of dealing with prices that end with 99p? Ask the children to use the back of this sheet to do their working out.

Name _____ Date _____

What do three cost?

Here is the price list from the sports shop:

SPORTS SHOP PRICES:

Badminton shuttlecocks (three pack)	£3.99
Badminton racket	£9.99
Basketball ring with net	£19.99
Basketball	£4.99
Football	£4
Goalkeeper's gloves	£6.99
Football goal	£40
Junior tennis racket	£14.99
Tennis balls (four pack)	£4.99
Netball post with net	£55
Netball	£3

What do 3 badminton rackets cost altogether?

What do 3 basketball rings altogether?

What do 3 packs of tennis balls cost altogether?

What do 3 packs of shuttlecocks cost altogether?

What do 3 junior tennis rackets cost altogether?

Teacher's notes

Suggested objective: *Solve one-step and two-step problems involving money.*

Problem: *What do three cost?*

Look at the sports items on sheet 89 with the children. Can they think of a quick way of dealing with prices that end with 99p? Ask the children to use the back of this sheet to do their working out.

How many ways can you make £10?

£10

£5

Here are the notes and coins you can use:

How many ways can you make £10 using only the coins and notes shown? Some ways are shown for you below. How many other ways can you find?

£2 £1

£10	1 x £10
£10	10 x £1
£10	
£10	
£10	
£10	
£10	
£10	
£10	

Teacher's notes

Suggested objective: *Devise a strategy for finding all ways of making a total of £10.*

Problem: *How many ways can you make £10?*
Ask individual children to make £10, using only the coins and notes shown. There are only nine ways of making £10. Do the children work methodically? Do they make and use lists and tables to organise and interpret their information? Do they identify patterns?

Name _____ Date _____

Discussion sheet: What is the temperature?

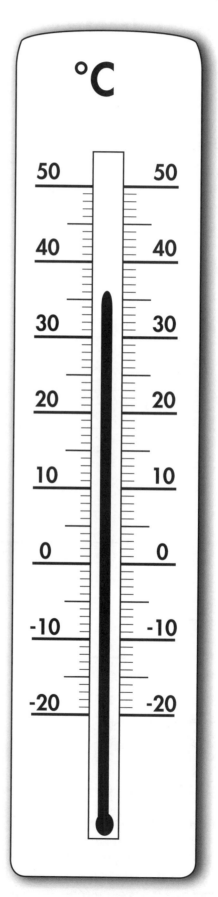

Teacher's notes

Suggested objective:
Interpret intervals and divisions on partially numbered scales.

Problem: *What is the temperature?*
Discuss the thermometer with the children, firstly considering the numbered markings. What is the temperature like outside today? Which of the numbered markings would that be closest to? Point at various markings and support the children in identifying the temperatures shown – look at positive temperatures first, then explain how the temperatures below zero are marked.
When you feel that the children are confident, give them the first of the thermometer activity sheets.

What are the temperatures?

Write the correct temperatures in the boxes.

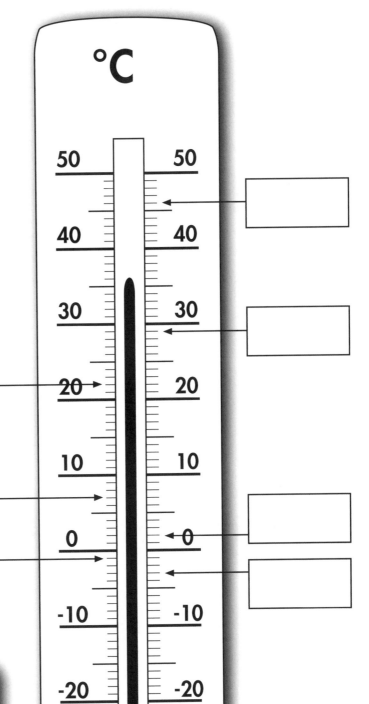

Andrew Brodie: Solving Maths Problems 7–9 © A&C Black 2010

What are the differences in temperature?

The thermometer shows the temperatures in four cities of the UK one day in May.

How much warmer was the temperature in London than in Edinburgh?

How much cooler was the temperature in Cardiff than in Belfast?

How much warmer was the temperature in Belfast than in Edinburgh?

How much cooler was Belfast than London?

Write the four cities in order of temperature. Write the coolest first.

1. _____   3. _____

2. _____   4. _____

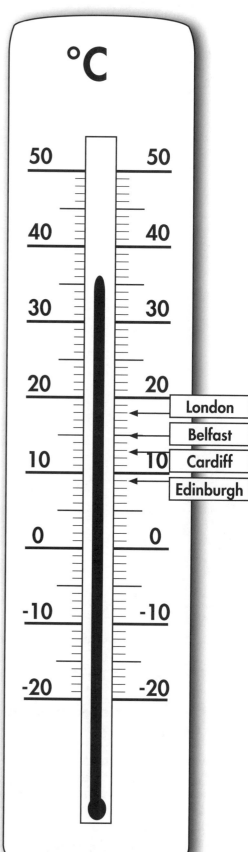

What are the differences in temperature?

The thermometer shows the temperatures in four cities of the United Kingdom one day in January.

How much warmer was the temperature in Edinburgh than in London?

How much cooler was the temperature in Cardiff than in Belfast?

How much warmer was the temperature in Edinburgh than in Belfast?

How much warmer was London than Cardiff?

Write the four cities in order of temperature. Write the coolest first.

1._____   3._____

2._____   4._____

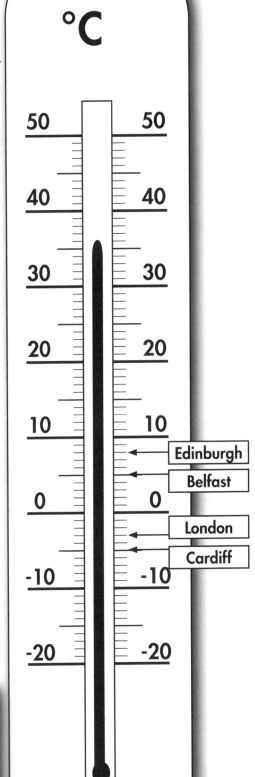

Teacher's notes

Suggested objective: *Interpret intervals and divisions on partially numbered scales.*

Problem: *What are the differences in temperature?*
The children should be able to identify the indicated temperatures, then make comparisons between them. Why are they so different to the temperatures shown on sheet 98?

Andrew Brodie: Solving Maths Problems 7–9 © A&C Black 2010

What are the differences in temperature?

The thermometer shows the temperatures in four cities of the world one day in January.

How much warmer was the temperature in Nairobi than in London?

How much cooler was the temperature in London than in Sydney?

How much warmer was the temperature in Nairobi than in Sydney?

How much warmer was London than Moscow?

Write the four cities in order of temperature. Write the coolest first.

1. _____   3. _____

2. _____   4. _____

°C

50   50

40   40

← Nairobi

30   30

← Sydney

20   20

10   10

0 ← 0   London

-10   -10

← Moscow

-20   -20

Teacher's notes

Suggested objective: *Interpret intervals and divisions on partially numbered scales.*

Problem: *What are the differences in temperature?*
The children should be able to identify the indicated temperatures, then make comparisons between them.

Temperatures on a bar chart

The bar chart shows the temperatures that were recorded in Birmingham every day for a week.

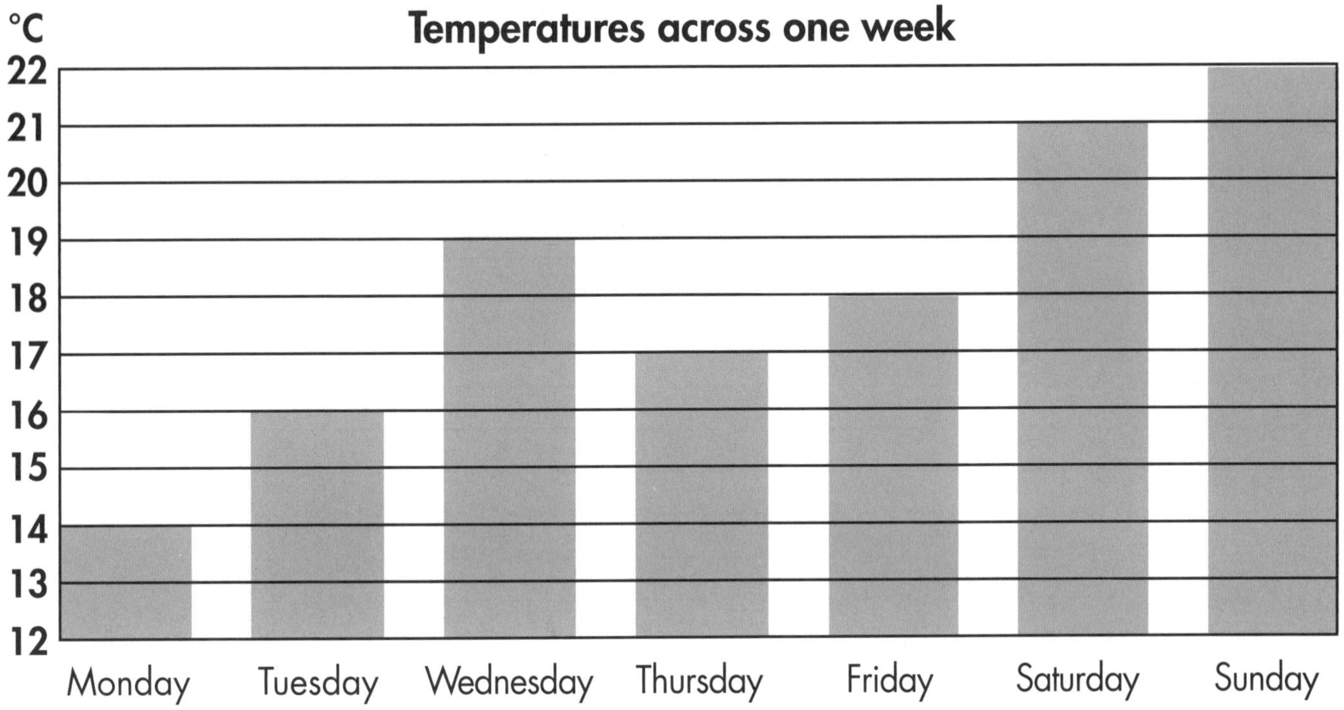

Temperatures across one week

°C

Monday	Tuesday	Wednesday	Thursday	Friday	Saturday	Sunday

Which day had the coolest temperature? ☐

How much warmer was Saturday than Thursday? ☐

Which day had the warmest temperature? ☐

How much cooler was Tuesday than Wednesday? ☐

How much warmer was the warmest day than the coldest day? ☐

Teacher's notes

Suggested objective: *Interpret data on a bar chart.*

Problem: *What temperatures are recorded on the bar chart?*
The children should be able to identify the recorded temperatures, then make comparisons between them.
Extension Problem: Do you think these temperatures were recorded in Spring, Summer, Autumn or Winter? Do the children notice that the temperature axis does not start at zero?

Comparing temperatures on a bar chart

The bar chart shows the temperatures that were recorded at exactly the same time but in different cities across the world.

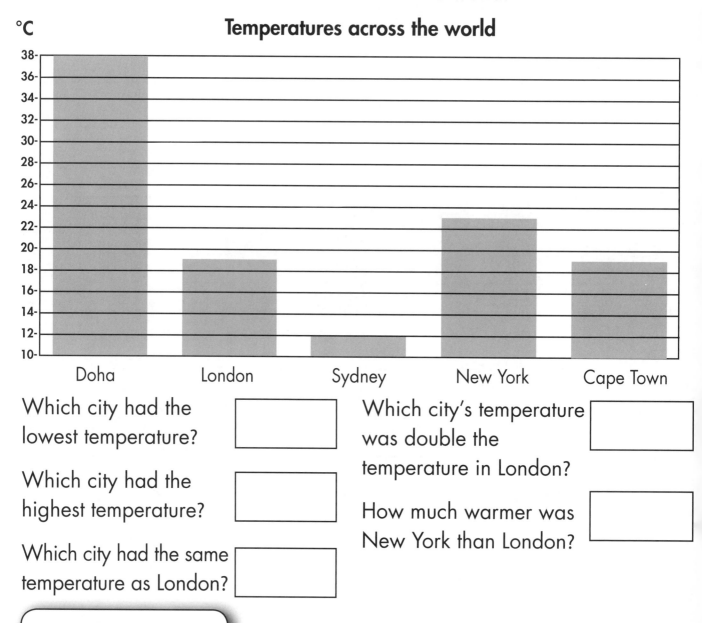

Which city had the lowest temperature?

Which city had the highest temperature?

Which city had the same temperature as London?

Which city's temperature was double the temperature in London?

How much warmer was New York than London?

Can you make a cube from its net?

Teacher's notes

Suggested objective: *Begin to recognise nets of familiar shapes.*

Problem: *Can you make a cube from its net?*

Ask the children to cut out the net of a cube. This sheet serves as an introduction to sheet 104, where pupils have to find the diagram that does not represent the net of a cube. Their manipulation of the net on this sheet will help them in their understanding of nets of solid shapes.

Name _____ Date _____

Which net doesn't make a cube?

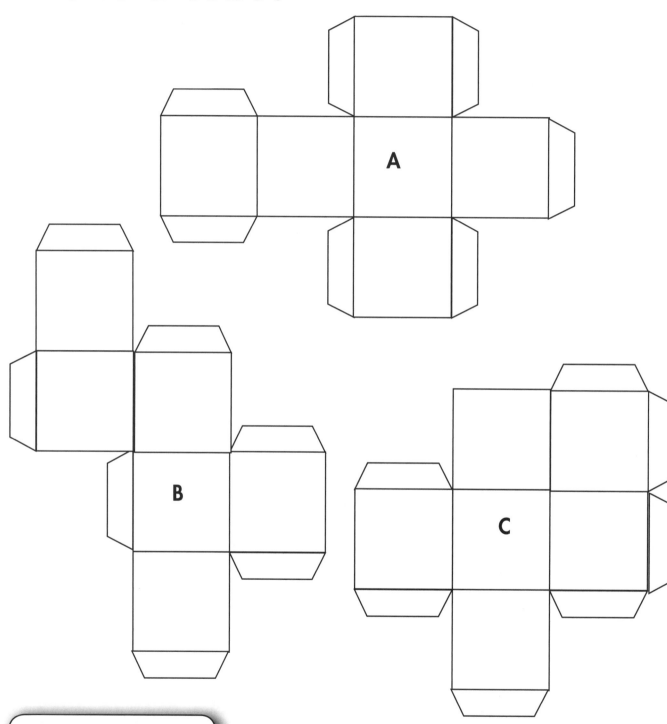

Teacher's notes

Suggested objective: *Begin to recognise nets of familiar shapes.*

Problem: *Which net doesn't make a cube?*
Pupils should attempt this investigation after completing the practical activity of making a cube on sheet 103.

What shapes can you find?

What other shapes can you find by drawing a straight line from one corner of a **heptagon** to another corner?

What different shapes do you find when you draw a line from the same corner as above but to a different corner?

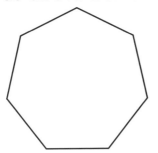 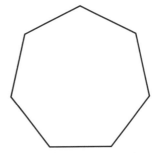

What shapes can you find if you draw more than one line? Investigate with these heptagons:

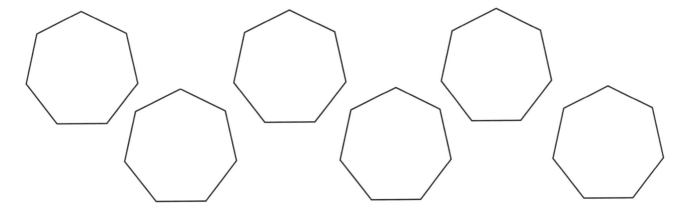

Teacher's notes

Suggested objective: *Investigate shapes and use correct vocabulary.*

Problem: *What shapes can you find?*
Encourage the children to investigate by drawing lines. As with all good investigations there are no right or wrong results – every result should be considered as valid and should encourage useful discussion.

What shapes can you find?

What other shapes can you find by drawing a straight line from one corner of a **nonagon** to another corner?

What different shapes do you find when you draw a line from the same corner as above but to a different corner?

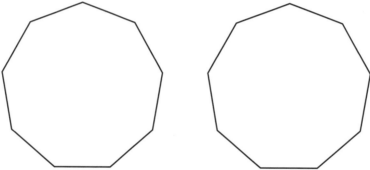

What shapes can you find if you draw more than one line? Investigate with these nonagons:

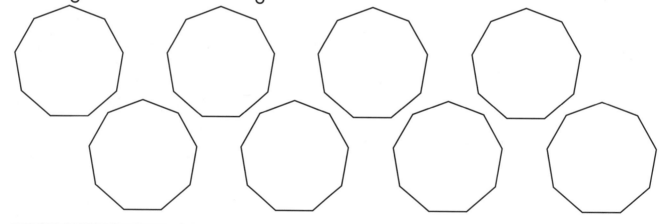

Teacher's notes

Suggested objective: *Investigate shapes and use correct vocabulary.*

Problem: *What shapes can you find?*

Encourage the children to investigate by drawing lines. As with all good investigations there are no right or wrong results every result should be considered as valid and should encourage useful discussion.

Andrew Brodie: Solving Maths Problems 7–9 © A&C Black 2010

Name _____ Date _____

What time is it?

What time does the clock show?

What time will it be 12 minutes after this time?

What time does the clock show?

What time was it 22 minutes before this time?

What time does the clock show?

What time will it be 7 minutes after this time?

Teacher's notes

Suggested objective: *Interpret times shown on the partially numbered scale on a clock.*

Problem: *What time is it?*
The children need to interpret the wording of each question then use the appropriate vocabulary or number representation to show the correct time and the related time as asked by the question.

What time is it?

What time does the clock show?

What time will it be 14 minutes after this time?

What time does the clock show?

What time was it 16 minutes before this time?

What time does the clock show?

What time will it be 23 minutes after this time?

Teacher's notes

Suggested objective: *Interpret times shown on the partially numbered scale on a clock.*

Problem: *What time is it?*
The children need to interpret the wording of each question then use the appropriate vocabulary or number representation to show the correct time and the related time as asked by the question.
Extension activity: Ask the children to continue the time differences for each clock. For example, with the first clock ask them to keep adding 12 minutes to each time that they find can they successfully find the time where it crosses the hour?

What are the time differences? Sheet 109

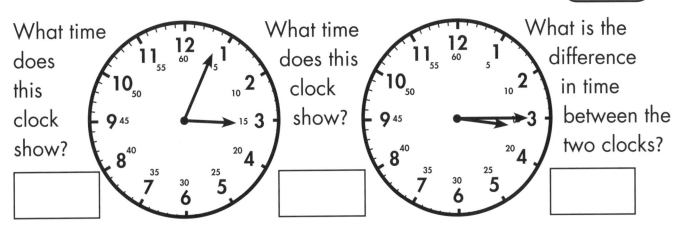

What time does this clock show?

[ ]

What time does this clock show?

[ ]

What is the difference in time between the two clocks?

[ ]

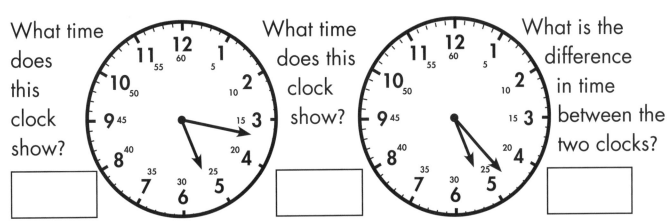

What time does this clock show?

[ ]

What time does this clock show?

[ ]

What is the difference in time between the two clocks?

[ ]

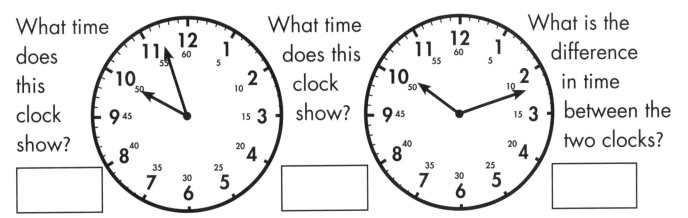

What time does this clock show?

[ ]

What time does this clock show?

[ ]

What is the difference in time between the two clocks?

[ ]

Teacher's notes

Suggested objective: *Interpret times shown on the partially numbered scale on a clock.*

Problem: *What are the time differences?*
The children need to use the appropriate vocabulary or number representation to show the correct number of minutes between the times on each pair of clocks.

Extension activity: Ask the children to continue the time differences for each clock. For example, with the first clock ask them to keep adding 12 minutes to each time that they find can they successfully find the time where it crosses the hour?

When do the bus companies match in time?

A red bus leaves the bus station at 7am. Red buses leave every 15 minutes after that.

A green bus leaves the bus station at 7am. Green buses leave every 12 minutes after that.

Fill in the chart below to show the times the next 10 red buses and the next 10 green buses leave the bus station.

Red Bus Company		Green Bus Company	
07.00		07.00	

At what times do both bus companies have buses leaving the bus station together?

Teacher's notes

Suggested objective: *Look for patterns in the results.*

Problem: *When do the bus companies match in time?*
Ensure that the children understand the situation: explain that buses from two different bus companies both share the same bus station. Both have buses leaving at 7am. The children could use vocabulary such as 'how frequently', 'more frequently', etc.

When do the bus companies match in time?

A small bus leaves the bus station at 7am. Small buses leave every 8 minutes after that.

A big bus leaves the bus station at 7am. Big buses leave every 18 minutes after that.

Fill in the chart below to show the times the next 10 small buses and the next 10 big buses leave the bus station.

Small Bus Company		Big Bus Company	
07.00		07.00	

At what times do both bus companies have buses leaving the bus station together?

Teacher's notes

Suggested objective: *Look for patterns in the results.*

Problem: *When do the bus companies match in time?*
Extension problem: Look back at the times for the red buses and the green buses on Sheet 110. At what time will all four bus companies have buses leaving the bus station?

Andrew Brodie: Solving Maths Problems 7–9 © A&C Black 2010

Name _____ Date _____

Discussion sheet: How do the distances compare?

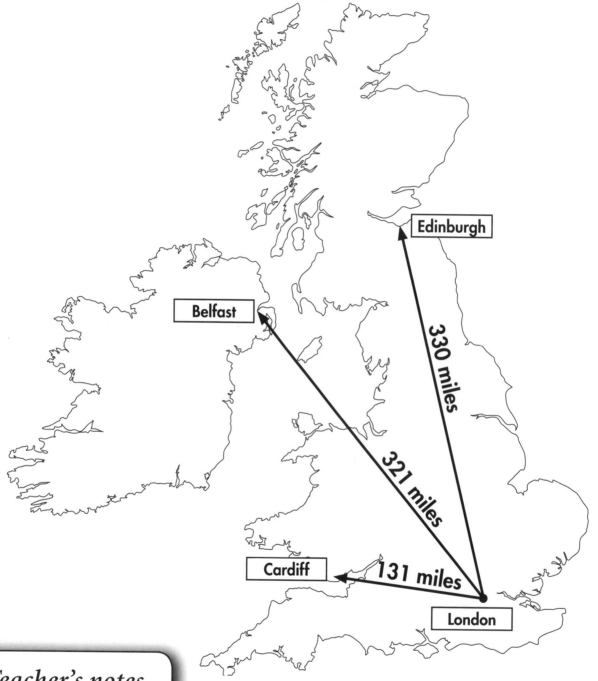

Teacher's notes

Suggested objective: *Solve one-step and two-step problems involving measures.*

Problem: *How do the distances compare?*

Discuss the map with the children. Point out that the arrows are straight indicating that the distances shown are 'as the crow flies'. Ask the children to compare the distances from London to the three other cities. Which city is closest? Which city is furthest away? Why might it take longer to get to Belfast than to Edinburgh if travelling by road?

How do the distances compare?

How much further is it from London to Edinburgh than from London to Belfast?

How much further is it from London to Edinburgh than from London to Cardiff?

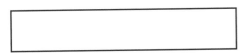

How much further is it from London to Belfast than from London to Cardiff?

If it were possible to travel in a straight line, how far would it be from London to Edinburgh then back again?

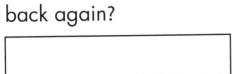

If it were possible to travel in a straight line, how far would it be from London to Belfast then back again?

If it were possible to travel in a straight line, how far would it be from London to Cardiff then back again?

Teacher's notes

This sheet to be used in conjunction with Discussion sheet 112.
Suggested objective: *Solve one-step and two-step problems involving measures.*

Problem: *How do the distances compare?*
Look at the map on sheet 112 with the children. Ask children to answer the questions above.

How do the distances compare?

The actual distances from London to the other cities when travelling by road are:

London to Edinburgh:
407 miles by road.

London to Belfast: 467 miles by road (with a ferry crossing).

London to Cardiff:
152 miles by road.

How much further is it to Edinburgh by road than 'as the crow flies'?

How much further is it to Belfast by road and ferry than 'as the crow flies'?

How much further is it to Cardiff by road than 'as the crow flies'?

For which city has the travelling distance increased the most?

Teacher's notes

This sheet to be used in conjunction with Discussion sheet 112.
Suggested objective: *Solve one-step and two-step problems involving measures.*

Problem: *How do the distances compare?*
Look at the map on sheet 112 and the actual distances with the children. Ask the children to answer the questions above. Discuss the road distances and why these are longer than the direct routes.

How many miles do I travel?

IRISH

The actual distances from London to the other cities when travelling by road are:

London to Edinburgh: 407 miles by road.

London to Belfast: 467 miles by road (with a ferry crossing).

London to Cardiff: 152 miles by road.

If I drive to Edinburgh and back, how many miles do I drive?

If I drive to Belfast and back, how many miles do I drive?

If I drive to Cardiff and back, how many miles do I drive?

If I drive to Cardiff and back to London every week for ten weeks, how many miles have I driven on this route altogether?

If I drive to Edinburgh and back to London every week for ten weeks, how many miles have I driven on this route altogether?

How many miles have I driven on the Cardiff and Edinburgh routes altogether over the ten weeks?

Teacher's notes

This sheet to be used in conjunction with Discussion sheet 112.
Suggested objective: *Solve one-step and two-step problems involving measures.*

Problem: *How many miles do I travel?*
Look at the distances with the children. Remind them of the need to double these when finding the lengths of the return journeys. Do they remember the effect of multiplying by 10?

Name _____ Date _____

What numbers fit in the gaps?

Look carefully at the puzzle. It has a target number of 6.

You need to write some numbers to make a subtraction, a multiplication and an addition sentence all with the answer 6.

Here are the numbers you must use: 2, 2, 3, 4, 5 and 11.

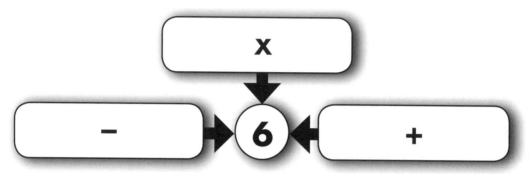

Look carefully at the next puzzle. You need to find the target number that goes in the middle and you need to write numbers in the correct places to make a subtraction, addition and multiplication sentence.

The numbers you must use are: 3, 4, 5, 5, 7, 12 and 17.

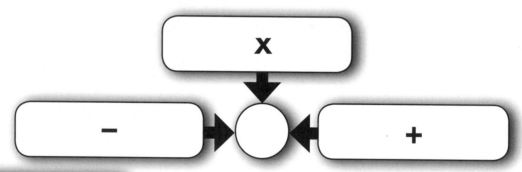

Teacher's notes

Suggested objective: *Identify patterns and relationships involving numbers.*

Problem: *Can you find the numbers to fill the gaps?*
Do the children use mental recall of addition and subtraction facts? Do they adopt a systematic approach? Do they make connections and apply their knowledge to similar situations? Do they present solutions to puzzles and problems in an organized way? Can they describe and explain methods, choices and solutions to puzzles and problems?

What numbers fit in the gaps?
Sheet 117

Look carefully at the puzzle below. It has a target number of 12.

You need to wite some numbers to make a subtraction, a multiplication, a division and an addition sentence all with the answer 12.

Here are numbers you must use: 2, 2, 4, 6, 6, 8, 18, 24.

Write them in the correct places on the puzzle.

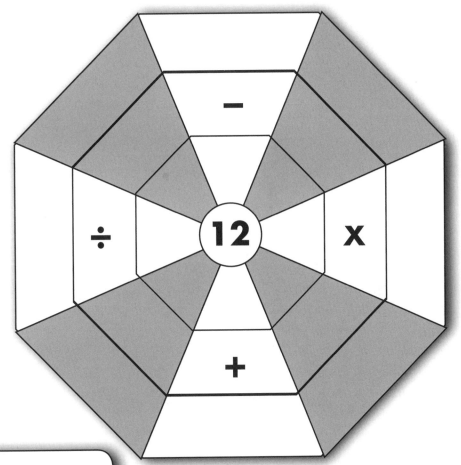

Teacher's notes

Suggested objective: *Identify patterns and relationships involving numbers.*

Problem: *Can you find the numbers to fill the gaps?*
Do the children use mental recall of addition and subtraction facts? Do they adopt a systematic approach? Do they make connections and apply their knowledge to similar situations? Do they present solutions to puzzles and problems in an organized way? Can they describe and explain methods, choices and solutions to puzzles and problems?

What numbers fit in the gaps?
Sheet 118

Look carefully at the puzzle below. You have to find the target number and complete the number sentences.

You need to write some numbers to make a subtraction, a multiplication, a division and an addition sentence.

Here are numbers you must use: 2, 4, 4, 4, 8, 12, 16, 24 and 32.

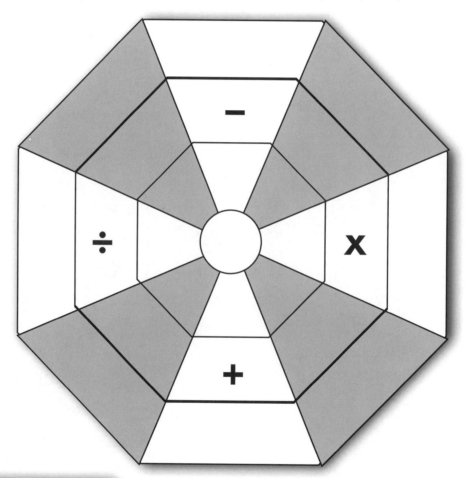

Teacher's notes

Suggested objective: *Identify patterns and relationships involving numbers.*

Problem: *Can you find the numbers to fill the gaps?*

Do the children use mental recall of addition and subtraction facts? Do they adopt a systematic approach? Do they make connections and apply their knowledge to similar situations? Do they present solutions to puzzles and problems in an organized way? Can they describe and explain methods, choices and solutions to puzzles and problems?

Andrew Brodie: Solving Maths Problems 7–9 © A&C Black 2010